D1329083

WELCOME TO RUGBY LEGENDS

Lunar Press is a privately-run publishing company that cares greatly about its content's accuracy.

If you notice any inaccuracies or have anything that you would like to discuss in the book, then please email us at lunarpresspublishing@gmail.com.

Enjoy!

CONTENTS

KICK OFF

Welcome to our list of 20 of the world's greatest-ever rugby players. As you will see in the pages that follow, separating these guys (and the ones who just missed out!) would be impossible. That's why they aren't numbered, as doing so would be unfair. Like all sports, who we decide to be the greatest is a matter of opinion.

Some players have made the list because they won it all, while others changed the way rugby was played. Some, like Jonah Lomu, brought the sport to a new level, while others, such as Sergio Parisse, dominated while playing for a much weaker team. All of the players here deserve their spot, though. They are all legends of the game.

In these pages, we will cover generations of rugby, from the Welsh backline of the seventies that has yet to be equalled, to players such as Michael Hooper, who are still playing at the time of this book being written. History always changes, and records repeatedly get broken. These are the guys who made those kinds of differences. They are World Cup winners and Heineken Cup champions.

Throughout the history of rugby, only a handful of nations have dominated. But that dominance often switches hands for periods, and it was usually the players mentioned here who made that happen. Once in a while, a truly exceptional player comes along that changes the way we see a certain sport. Guys like David Campese and Jonny Wilkinson. Or Dan Carter and Gavin Hastings.

Then there are the mavericks, the players who make us get up off our seats when they get the ball. When Jonah Lomu flicked England's backline aside at the 1995 World Cup on his way to scoring four unbelievable tries, he was described as a "freight train in ballet shoes." That's how exceptional he was throughout his career. It was that game that brought the sport of rugby into the living rooms of the people who had never watched before. It made the news.

Others have had similar moments, like Jonny Wilkinson's kick with 26 seconds remaining to win the 2003 World Cup. After that, kids all over the world could be seen on their local pitches, their hands clasped in front of them as they eyed up the posts. They wanted to be Jonny Wilkinson, and that's the effect that true legends have.

Each and every one of the players you're about to read about made a difference in a positive way. Some of them continue to do so in retirement through their businesses or charity work. A few have passed on, and they'll be forever missed. One or two are still playing, so their stories are still being created!

Whatever the case may be, we hope you enjoy learning some cool things about them. You will know some of them, but a few of the older players might be new to you. So, turn the page and let yourself escape into the wonderful world of rugby legends!

JONAH LOMU

INTERNATIONAL CAREER

DEBUT	1994
CAPS	63
WINS	44
TRIES	37
POINTS	185

WORLD CUP STATS

DEBUT	1995
TOURNAMENTS	2
CAPS	11
TRIES	15
TITLES	0

BIOGRAPHY

BORN	12 MAY 1975
NATIONALITY	NEW ZEALANDER
POSITION(S)	WING, NUMBER 8
HEIGHT	1.92 M (6 FT 4 IN)
RETIRED	2007

Widely considered to be the most electrifying player in the history of rugby, Jonah Lomu is a true legend. He is also the player who brought the sport to the attention of even non-rugby fans. His speed, mixed with his immense power, was unheard of, and he struck fear into every defence he faced.

He died far too soon, but he will always be remembered as the biggest draw rugby has ever known.

Jonah Lomu's childhood wasn't easy, but he came through it to become a superstar in one of the toughest sports on the planet. He was born in Pukekohe, a small town in Auckland, on 12 May 1975. His parents had emigrated from Tonga, and they struggled financially. Jonah spent a lot of his early years between his home in Pukekohe and the house of his auntie and uncle back in Holopeka, a small village on the islands of Ha'apai, just off Tonga.

His parents finally settled in the Auckland suburb of Mangere, where Jonah was surrounded by gang violence and murder. He grew up poor but loved. With all the negativity around him, he found positivity in sports.

Despite the safety inside his childhood home, the streets were always dangerous. Jonah lost his uncle and his cousin to gang violence before his teens, but his mother saved everything she could to get him out. She succeeded and somehow managed to pay for his tuition at Wesley College in Auckland. Once there, he excelled, especially in sports.

Jonah was brilliant at many different sports, including the high jump, javelin, shot put, relay, hurdles, 100 metres and, of course, rugby. In his time there, he recorded an 11.2-second sprint in the 100 metres! That's close to world record stuff!

Of all the sports he dominated, rugby was the one he preferred. And it's not surprising, given his skill set. He used his talent in the high jump, relay and sprinting to hone his rugby skills. And we need to remember that Jonah Lomu grew to six-foot-four and 120 kilograms (18 stone 13 pounds), so he was a big teenager! A boy of that size running full speed must have been a terrifying sight for the opposing players!

One of the most important moments in his life came at the age of fourteen when he was asked to play in a game of touch rugby organised by Rugby Sevens legend Eric Rush. Lomu was so dominant that Rush asked him to get on a plane the following day to play in a tournament that was taking place in Singapore. Jonah agreed and brushed everyone aside in the competition.

But Sevens wasn't the type of rugby for Jonah. As much as he enjoyed it, he wanted to play rugby union, and specifically international Test rugby. He soon got his chance.

Originally, Lomu played as an openside flanker, usually number 7. He was soon switched to the left wing (the position we all remember him for), and everything changed. He was unstoppable.

His rise up the ranks was fast. He played for the New Zealand under-19 side in 1993 and graduated to the under-21s the following year. Then, only a month after turning 19, he became the youngest New Zealand Test player in history when he played against France. The All Blacks lost the game (8–22), but Lomu impressed.

After just two caps, he was included in the New Zealand squad for the 1995 Rugby World Cup in South Africa. It was here that he would become global news, and footage of his demolition of England in the semifinals would go viral before viral was even a thing!

Lomu scored two tries in the opening match against Ireland as New Zealand won all three of their games in Pool C. He followed this up with another try against Scotland in the quarterfinals to set up a mouthwatering clash with England in the semis at the Newlands Stadium in Cape Town.

England knew little about the kid in the All Blacks team called Jonah Lomu. Even if they'd changed their tactics to stop him, it wouldn't have made a difference. Not that day. Jonah Lomu was on fire throughout the match, flicking tackles off him like flies as he barged through the English defence.

His first try set the tone, and it is often remembered as the greatest try of all time. Picking up a loose pass that had bounced behind him, he turned to face the

English defence. He palmed off two players as if they were nothing before steamrolling through England's usually unbreakable Mike Catt. He touched the ball down and jogged back, barely celebrating one of rugby's golden moments.

Will Carling, an English legend, was stunned after the game by what he saw. He praised Lomu, saying that he was a freak of nature and basically unstoppable. Seeing how Lomu scored another three tries after that one to demolish the English, it's easy to agree!

New Zealand faced South Africa in the final. If the Springboks hadn't had a plan to stop Lomu before the All Blacks beat England, they did now. They locked up, restricting New Zealand to kicks and lineouts. A drab final saw no tries, and South Africa scraped a 15–12 win to lift the trophy.

The first-ever Tri Nations was played in 1996, involving South Africa, New Zealand and Australia. (Argentina became a part of it in 2009.) New Zealand won it at the first time of asking, completing a clean sweep, including a 43–6 demolition of arch-rivals Australia. Lomu scored another wonder try in the game.

A year that started so well ended in sadness for Jonah Lomu and his family. He was diagnosed with a rare and serious kidney disorder. He had to walk away from the sport he loved to concentrate on his recovery.

Amazingly, Lomu returned to rugby in 1998 and even led New Zealand to the gold at the Commonwealth

Games in Kuala Lumpur. But his form was still far from his best, and in his absence from the national team, Lomu had lost his place in the starting XV. He came off the bench in all of the 1999 World Cup warm-up games and won his place back in time for the opening match.

Lomu was sensational again, scoring 8 tries in the tournament, bringing his total to 15. It was the most scored by a single player in World Cup history until Bryan Habana equalled it. We will cover Habana later in the book!

Jonah Lomu's career was stop-start until he retired in 2005. His illness worsened, and he needed a kidney transplant in 2004. Somehow, he played again after this, but his appearances were sporadic*.

Jonah Lomu died in 2015 from a heart attack. His heart had been severely weakened over the years due to his illness, but he fought with everything he had to beat it. He will always be remembered as the most watchable, powerful and entertaining player ever to pick up a rugby ball.

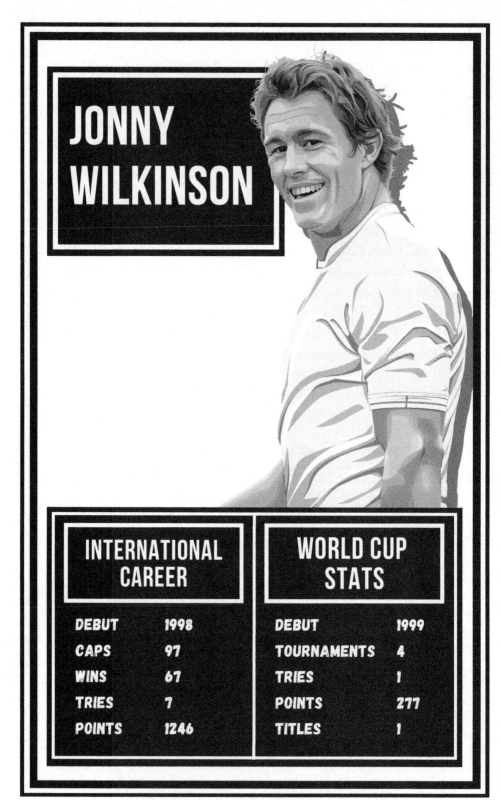

JONNY WILKINSON

INTERNATIONAL CAREER

DEBUT	1998
CAPS	97
WINS	67
TRIES	7
POINTS	1246

WORLD CUP STATS

DEBUT	1999
TOURNAMENTS	4
TRIES	1
POINTS	277
TITLES	1

International stats include matches for the British & Irish Lions

BIOGRAPHY

BORN	25 MAY 1979
NATIONALITY	ENGLISH
POSITION(S)	FLY-HALF
HEIGHT	1.78 M (5 FT 10 IN)
RETIRED	2014

Now we have another serial winner and, like Jonah Lomu, someone who suffered a lot with injuries. Rugby is a tough sport—probably the most physical in the world after boxing and UFC—so the men and women who play for years often damage their bodies. Jonny Wilkinson never gave less than 100%, even when he wasn't feeling the best. He is a rugby legend and a player who won it all.

The man who would grow up to be one of, if not England's greatest-ever fly-half was born in Farnham, Surrey, in 1979. He grew up surrounded by rugby. His father was a good player who became a coach, and he helped develop Jonny's game as a kid. Not that young Wilkinson needed much help. He was a natural, and very early on, there was talk that he might one day be an England international.

Jonny did well at school, and studying came naturally to him. He could have gone on to many colleges, but the call of rugby was too much. It was all he ever wanted to do, so when he was offered a place at Durham University, he turned it down. He wanted to concentrate solely on rugby.

Throughout his childhood, Jonny played many different positions, including long stints at inside centre. But he always came back to where he belonged, at fly-half and kicker. The second of these was what would make him famous. Jonny Wilkinson is often considered the greatest kicker in history.

Jonny got his professional breakthrough in 1997 when he signed for the Newcastle Falcons. Jonny was clearly a star in the making, but he still had some areas of his game that needed polishing. His kicking was already good, but it was becoming world-class. And he filled out. Originally quite a skinny kid, he began to pile on mass on his way to the 89 kilograms (14 stone) of his professional days. At just five-foot-ten, he needed to be strong to look after himself on the rugby pitch.

By 1998, he was already making his mark in the rugby world when he won the Allied Dunbar Premiership. It was the first time the Newcastle Falcons had ever won it. His performances for the Falcons earned Jonny his first England call-up, but he was an unused substitute in the game against Scotland. He did make his debut in the following game, though, coming on for the legendary Mike Catt. Jonny was only 18 years old.

His joy at becoming a full international was short-lived. That game was quickly followed by what is now known as the "Tour of Hell." England travelled to the southern hemisphere, where they were demolished by Australia and New Zealand. Their loss to the Kiwis was the worst of all—a 0–76 thrashing.

Back at Newcastle, Rob Andrew retired from playing to become a coach. This freed up the position of fly-half, meaning Wilko was able to nail down a starting spot in his favourite position. It is considered a huge moment in Jonny's career, and he flourished.

By 1999, Jonny had also secured his starting spot for England, playing in all four of their Five Nations games. He followed this up by playing for England at the 1999 World Cup in Wales. Jonny performed brilliantly, scoring a try in the opening game against Italy. He added to this with six conversions and five penalty goals. In total, he scored 32 points in his first World Cup game!

He played the next match against New Zealand, converting a try and scoring three penalties, but England lost. He was rested against Tonga (a 101–10 win for England) before being brought back for the quarterfinal playoff game against Fiji, which England won.

In a shock move by head coach Clive Woodward, Jonny was dropped for the quarterfinal against South Africa, and England were knocked out. Woodward was asked some serious questions when the team returned home. Jonny Wilkinson was already a fan favourite, and the public wanted answers!

Jonny kept his head down and let his skills on the pitch do the talking. He led England to the 2000 Six Nations. This was the first year that Italy had become part of the tournament, and Jonny played in all five England games. They won it again in 2001, with Jonny setting a new record for points in a single game (35 against Italy at Twickenham).

He had a fantastic 2001 where he also won the Powergen Cup with Newcastle. He was also selected as fly-half/kicker for the British Lions' tour of Australia.

But 2003 was the year that was all about Jonny Wilkinson. It was the year when he would write himself into the history books and create many magical moments, none more memorable than his kick with 26 seconds left on the clock at the Stadium Australia, Sydney.

First of all, he led England to the Grand Slam at the Six Nations. England were still licking their wounds from the 1999 World Cup defeat to South Africa, and they felt that this was the year when they could finally get their hands on the Webb Ellis Cup. Doing the Grand Slam in the Six Nations was the perfect way to announce themselves as one of the favourites.

England were drawn in Pool B alongside South Africa, which only added to the story. After a dominant 84–6 win over Georgia, England got revenge on the Springboks by hammering them 25–6. Wilkinson scored 20 of England's points, confirming that being dropped four years before had been a huge mistake. They beat Samoa, meaning Jonny could be rested for the final group game with no risk of not winning the pool.

He was immense again in the quarterfinals, scoring 23 points in a 28–17 win over Wales. England then beat rugby giants France in the semifinal (24–7), with Wilko kicking every single point!

The final was expected to be epic, and those predictions proved correct. England faced Australia, who were the hosts, the holders and firm favourites. Still, England had Jonny Wilkinson, and the Wallabies had nobody of his class when it came to kicking.

A back-and-forth match saw the teams level at the final whistle. Extra time was needed, and with 26 seconds left on the clock, Jonny Wilkinson kicked the winner. It sparked huge celebrations, and a moment in time had been created by England's star player. It was the first game Australia had lost at the World Cup in eight years.

Wilkinson finished the tournament with 113 points. He was named BBC Sports Personality of the Year and the 2003 IRB Player of the Year.

But only weeks after the World Cup, the injury problems that would plague him for the rest of his career began. He played just 937 minutes of the next 18 months of rugby. Then, just 47 minutes into his second game after being out, he tore the ligaments in his right knee. Lacerated kidneys, more knee issues and a string of other injuries continued to stall his progress.

His problems continued into England's defence of their World Cup in 2007, but he still put in some solid performances. He scored all 12 points in a 12–10 win over Australia, which saw him become the World Cup's highest points scorer. England reached the final again, and Jonny kicked all of England's six points. Unfortunately, they couldn't find the win. South Africa took it 15–6 to lift their second World Cup.

Jonny wasn't finished, at least at club level. After 12 years at Newcastle, he joined French side Toulon in 2009. He stayed there for five years, winning the Heineken Cup in 2013 and again in 2014. He scored 1,884 points in 141 games for Toulon and retired from all forms of rugby in 2014.

England's greatest-ever player? Some would say so. At the very least, Jonny Wilkinson is England's greatest-ever fly-half.

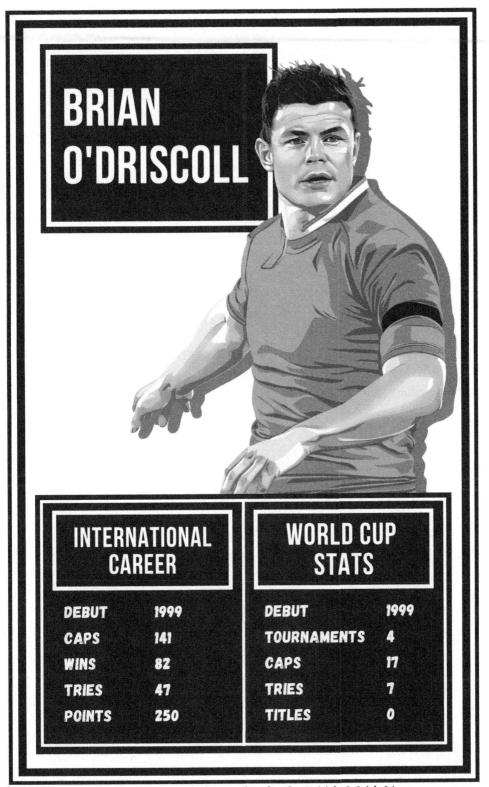

BRIAN O'DRISCOLL

INTERNATIONAL CAREER

DEBUT	1999
CAPS	141
WINS	82
TRIES	47
POINTS	250

WORLD CUP STATS

DEBUT	1999
TOURNAMENTS	4
CAPS	17
TRIES	7
TITLES	0

International stats include matches for the British & Irish Lions

BIOGRAPHY

BORN	21 JANUARY 1979
NATIONALITY	IRISH
POSITION(S)	OUTSIDE CENTRE
HEIGHT	1.78 M (5 FT 10 IN)
RETIRED	2014

A one-club man and the fourth-most capped international player in history, Brian O'Driscoll is an Irish legend. He led his country to two Six Nations, and as an outside centre, there haven't been many better in the game.

Born on 21 January 1979 in Dublin, Brian grew up surrounded by rugby. His father, Frank, played for Ireland, and so did two of his cousins. Both of his parents were doctors, and Brian grew up wanting for nothing. But he had a strict regime when it came to studying, and he carried that discipline into his rugby.

As a kid, Brian also played Gaelic football, but it was always rugby that was closest to his heart. When he started at Blackrock College as a teenager, his youth career really took off. Blackrock is a secondary school in Dublin that is famous for producing top rugby players. Brian played brilliantly, but he was often overlooked at the Irish youth level.

After secondary school, he attended the University College Dublin (UCD) on a scholarship and graduated with a diploma in Sports Management in 1998. Throughout his time in college, he played for Ireland's under-19s and under-21s. He was starting to gain a reputation as one of the most promising players in the country.

The following year (1999) saw Brian make a move that would change his life forever and set him on the path to becoming a club legend. He signed a contract with Leinster, the team where he would spend his whole career. It would also turn out to be a very important moment in Leinster's history. While there, he formed an impressive partnership with Shane Horgan, which they would carry on into the Ireland team over the coming years.

Brian made his Ireland debut in '99 against Australia in Brisbane. Although his first Test ended in defeat, he had made his mark and would be a mainstay in the Ireland setup for the next decade and a half.

By 2000, Brian was the star man in a very good Ireland side. At that year's Six Nations, he scored a hat trick of tries against France in Paris, leading Ireland to their first win on French soil in nearly 30 years! He followed this up the next year by winning the Celtic League with Leinster.

His impressive time with Ireland continued in 2002 when they beat Australia (18–9). It was the first time the Irish had beaten the Wallabies in over 20 years.

Brian O'Driscoll was the leader of the Leinster side that was becoming one of the most feared teams in Europe. They had always been considered quite a good team but not one of the elite. That was all going to change, and Leinster are still considered one of the greats today, and that's down to players like O'Driscoll and Horgan.

It all came together for Brian in the 2008–09 season.

Leinster won the Heineken Cup for the first time in their history, which sparked a period of European domination for the team. Brian also led Ireland to that year's Six Nations, picking up the Grand Slam and Triple Crown along the way.

Following a semifinal defeat in their defence of the Heineken Cup in the 2009–10 season, Leinster came back stronger in the 2010–11 season and reclaimed their title. They defended it again the following year, making it three Heineken Cups in four years. O'Driscoll was at the heart of everything they won.

As his international career wound down, Brian set a date for his retirement—the 2014 Six Nations. He played his last home game against Italy, contributing a hat trick of tries in a dominant win. He picked up the Man of the Match award while also winning his 140th Test cap, breaking the world record at the time.

His last-ever game for Ireland was against France in Paris. Ireland had only won once away to the French in 42 years. In a moment that was like something out of a movie, O'Driscoll drove the Irish on, battling like a man possessed. Ireland won the match, with the victory also giving them the Six Nations title.

On the pitch after the match, Brian was emotional. Still, he admitted there was no better way to bow out of international rugby.

In his time as a player, he won just about everything there was to win apart from the World Cup. His Leinster team of the late 2000s to early 2010s will always be regarded as one of the greatest, and his 133 caps for Ireland have cemented him as an all-time legend. He was a major part of the successful British & Irish Lions team that toured Australia and will always be in the conversation of who is the greatest-ever outside centre.

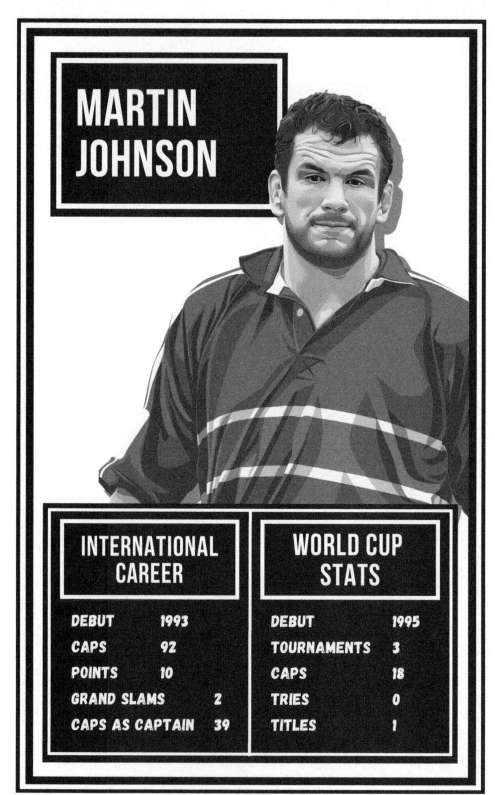

MARTIN JOHNSON

INTERNATIONAL CAREER

DEBUT	1993
CAPS	92
POINTS	10
GRAND SLAMS	2
CAPS AS CAPTAIN	39

WORLD CUP STATS

DEBUT	1995
TOURNAMENTS	3
CAPS	18
TRIES	0
TITLES	1

International stats include matches for the British & Irish Lions

BORN	9 MARCH 1970
NATIONALITY	ENGLISH
POSITION(S)	LOCK
HEIGHT	2.01 M (6 FT 7 IN)
RETIRED	2005

An absolute monster of a man, Martin Johnson was a rock in the England and Leicester teams in the nineties. Alongside his brother Will (he played for England and Leicester, too!), Martin Johnson won a string of medals during his career, including the 2003 World Cup. He is one of the best locks of all time and someone who represents everything good about English rugby.

Martin Johnson was born in Shirley in Solihull on 9 March 1970. He lived in Shirley until he was 7, when his family moved to Market Harborough, Leicestershire. It was a change in scenery that worked out well—Leicestershire is famed for producing world-class rugby players.

He attended Ridgeway Primary School, Welland Park Academy and Robert Smyth Academy during his time in Market Harborough. At each school, he excelled at rugby, among other sports. As he grew (he ended up at 6-foot-7!), rugby became his favourite sport. He was made for it, and he used every inch of that massive frame to carve out a career in the game he loved!

At the age of 19, Martin had attracted the attention of some of the world's biggest clubs, his reputation even stretching as far as New Zealand! King Country, one of New Zealand's oldest clubs, asked Martin to try out for them. He flew over, had a trial, and bossed it! They signed him on the spot.

In fact, he was so impressive that he was asked to play for the New Zealand under-21s. He agreed, but only for the practice. Martin Johnson was only ever going to play Test rugby for one team, and that was his native England. Still, touring Australia with some of the Kiwis' most promising players only helped develop his skills.

After his spell with King Country, he moved back home to sign for Leicester. He made his debut against an RAF select team, which was quickly followed by his Premiership debut against Bath. In what was then called the Courage League, Bath were the current champions and one of the best teams in Europe. They were also undefeated. The game was set up for a new star to be born.

Martin Johnson and the Leicester Tigers won 15–12, making his top-flight debut one to remember! It helped put him on the map, and he remained there for years to come!

Surprisingly, Martin didn't play for Leicester again for several months. He was still young, but it must have been frustrating sitting in the stands after such a fantastic debut. He waited and trained hard, finally getting his reward when he played his second game, this time in the Pilkington Cup. Remarkably, it was against the mighty Bath again! Even more remarkably, the Tigers won yet again!

By the 1992–93 season, he was one of Leicester's regulars. He helped them reach that year's Pilkington Cup final, where he scored a memorable try in a 23–16 victory over the Harlequins. He followed this up with his Test debut in the opening game of the 1993 Five Nations against France. Martin barely had time to prepare, getting called up for the squad at the last minute when Wade Dooley picked up an injury.

To make things even harder, he was knocked unconscious minutes into the game after a clash of heads with France's Laurent Seigne. The physios were adamant that Johnson should be subbed off, but he refused and played on to help England to a memorable 16–15 win. It was the type of bravery that made him a fan favourite in the years to come.

Despite his performance, Johnson was benched for the rest of Five Nations. Still, he had done enough to bring himself to the public's attention, and they were soon demanding he be included in future England First XVs. Martin finished his wonderful year with two appearances for the British & Irish Lions during their tour of New Zealand.

More success with the Leicester Tigers followed, which was made even more remarkable by the fact that Martin was working for Midland Bank the whole time. Rugby was yet to be made professional, and the players often had to work a second job to pay the bills! In August 1995, the Rugby Football Union (RFU) finally made rugby a professional sport, and Martin Johnson signed a new, well-paid contract. He quit his job at the bank the following day!

After signing his contract, his progress continued. He won the Courage League with Leicester in '95 and the Five Nations that same year. The second of these included the Grand Slam.

Martin was named captain of the Lions team that toured South Africa in 1997 and again in 2001 when they travelled throughout Australia. This made him the first player ever to captain the Lions on two separate tours. In between, he was named England captain, taking on the role in 1999. Martin Johnson's leadership skills have always been one of his strongest qualities, making him a world-class captain.

Leicester continued to dominate domestically, but success in Europe wasn't coming so easily. They lost to underdogs Brive in the Heineken Cup final in 1997, a result that stung for a long time. It wasn't until 2001 that they finally won their first-ever Heineken Cup, beating Stade Français 34–30 at the Parc des Princes. Johnson was so fired up that he was sent to the sin bin for punching Christophe Juillet, but his teammates managed to hold on and seal the victory.

The following season, the Tigers retained their title, becoming the first team in history to do so. They beat Munster in the final while also winning the league title, completing a superb double. Remember, Martin achieved all of this with his brother alongside him, making the success all the sweeter!

He saved his crowning moment for 2003 when he captained England to that historic World Cup win in Australia. In fact, that final turned out to be his last game for England. He played on at club level for another couple of years, but he was not the same player, and he retired in 2005.

After his playing career, he moved into coaching and managed England from 2008 to 2011. He led them to the Six Nations title, but the team never reached the heights it did while he was a player.

He will always be remembered as a rock in the England and Leicester sides, both of which made history with Martin Johnson at the heart of them.

SERGIO PARISSE

INTERNATIONAL CAREER

DEBUT	2002
CAPS	142
WINS	35
TRIES	16
POINTS	83

WORLD CUP STATS

DEBUT	2003
TOURNAMENTS	5
TRIES	3
POINTS	15
TITLES	0

BORN	12 SEPTEMBER 1983
NATIONALITY	ITALIAN / ARGENTINIAN
POSITION(S)	NUMBER EIGHT, FLANKER
HEIGHT	1.96 M (6 FT 5 IN)
RETIRED	STILL PLAYING

Italy have always been one of the underdogs in rugby. Through the years, they've had to settle for the odd victory in a sea of heavy losses, but they've always produced players who would die for the shirt. One man who has proved this more than any other is Sergio Parisse. He is not only Italy's greatest-ever player but one of the best flankers of any nation.

Sergio's career might have gone another way if he had chosen to play for the country of his birth. His father—also called Sergio—was an Italian national who played rugby for L'Aquila in Italy in the sixties and actually won the championship in his time there. But rugby, especially in countries outside of Britain and the southern hemisphere, wasn't very popular back then, and Sergio Snr had to work a second job to earn a wage.

This job was with the Alitalia airline, and when Sergio Snr was forced to move to Argentina to continue working, Buenos Aires became the Parisses' new home. And that's where Sergio Jnr was born on 12 September 1983.

Sergio Parisse grew up in Argentina, where the options to play rugby at the time weren't great. Still, he managed to make a name for himself, playing his junior rugby for Club Universitario de La Plata. By the late nineties, rugby had become more popular in

Argentina and Sergio's options grew. He was soon seen as the best young player in the country. The only problem for Argentina was that Sergio always knew he would play for Italy, the country of his parents!

By the time he was 19, Sergio felt that he had learned all he could in Buenos Aires, so he moved to Italy. He was quickly snapped up by Benetton Treviso and would go on to have four wonderful years there, winning the Serie A (now the Peroni Top 10) twice in his first few seasons.

Benetton Treviso were never going to be able to keep a player of Sergio's quality for too long, and Europe's bigger clubs soon came calling. Stade Français signed him in 2005, where he would go on to play the majority of his career. In his time with the Paris club (14 years), Sergio won two Top 14 titles and the European Challenge Cup twice.

Before all of this, young Sergio had been approached by both Argentina and Italy about representing them. In the end, there was never any other option for him than to play for Italy. At 17, he first appeared in the famous blue jersey for the Italian under-20 side at the Junior World Cup in Chile.

Sergio grew up speaking Italian at home, even in his years in Argentina. His parents were Italian, so it made sense. It was a decision that benefited the national side for years to come!

He made his Test debut at just 18. It was a baptism of fire*, as Sergio and the Gli Azzurri* came up against New Zealand. Italy lost 10–64, but Sergio really impressed, sometimes appearing to take on the whole Kiwi side on his own. This became a popular theme during Sergio's international career.

It was even more evident at the 2007 World Cup, where Italy failed to get past the pool stage. Once again, Sergio impressed while most of his teammates struggled. He would later claim that he wouldn't have changed anything about this situation, as Italy won and lost as a team. He loved playing for his country, and that was all that mattered.

The following year, at the 2008 Six Nations, Sergio won his 50th Test cap. He was only 24 years of age! Even more impressively, he was named team captain before the year was out. But these amazing feats weren't even the best part of 2008. At the end of the year, Sergio was nominated for the IRB Player of the Year, becoming the first Italian to do so. It was proof that he was a world-class player.

Unfortunately, the next couple of years were marred by injuries. This carried on through to 2010 when he missed the Six Nations. He recovered in time to captain his country at the 2011 World Cup in New Zealand, a competition where Italy made a major step forward compared to previous World Cups. They failed to make it to the knockout stage but were only a whisker away. Rugby's neutral fans were massively impressed.

Sergio's and Italy's improvements continued. Once seen as a team that just made up the numbers in any tournament they entered, they were starting to pick up a few massive results. None was more impressive than their 23–18 victory over France in the 2013 Six Nations, with Parisse scoring one of Italy's two tries. It was only the second time in their history beating the French.

They followed this up with another shock, defeating Ireland 22–15 in the final game. Italy finished fourth, ahead of both of the teams they beat!

Sergio signed for Toulon in 2019, where he has been for four seasons. He has begun to wind down his career at the time of this book being written, but still competes at the highest level. He played 142 times for Italy and is widely regarded as their greatest-ever player.

As Sergio's international career was coming to an end, one coach was asked how they could replace him when he finally hung up his boots. The answer was simple: You can't replace Sergio Parisse!

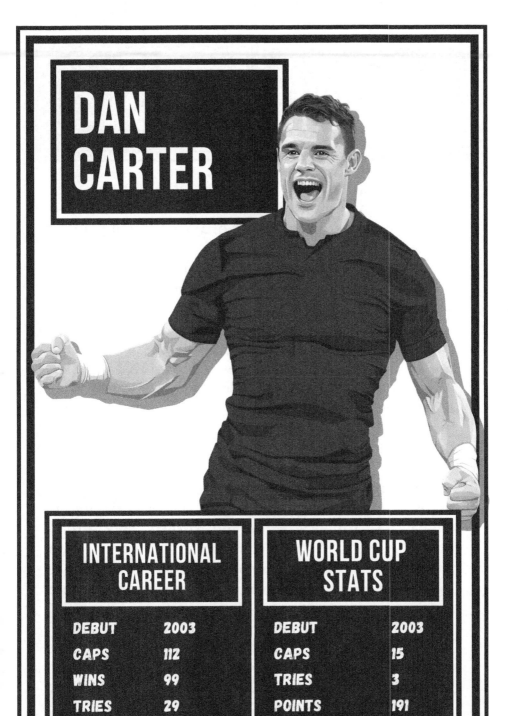

DAN CARTER

INTERNATIONAL CAREER

DEBUT	2003
CAPS	112
WINS	99
TRIES	29
POINTS	1598

WORLD CUP STATS

DEBUT	2003
CAPS	15
TRIES	3
POINTS	191
TITLES	2

BIOGRAPHY

BORN	5 MARCH 1982
NATIONALITY	NEW ZEALANDER
POSITION(S)	FLY-HALF
HEIGHT	1.78 M (5 FT 10 IN)
RETIRED	2021

A list of two World Cups, nine Tri Nations, five National Championships, and many more medals sounds like the trophy cabinet of a team full of players. But these are the accomplishments of just one man—a New Zealand legend who made the position of fly-half his own. Yep, it's safe to say there haven't been many players like Dan Carter!

On top of all these victories, Dan also scored 1,598 points in his Test match career, a record that cements him as one of the greatest ever to play the sport. With 112 caps for New Zealand, he is a national treasure, and his three Rugby Board Player of the Year awards equal the record set by Richie McCaw.

He grew up in Southbridge, South Island, and played rugby from an early age. At five, he was playing at halfback for his local team, and word quickly spread that there was a kid who could go all the way. Despite the constant praise that surrounded him, it's said that Dan always remained humble. In fact, some people said he was even quite shy.

Dan grew up with several role models in his life, none more so than his great-uncle, who played for New Zealand in the 1920s and was part of the famous Invincibles. Having such excellence to live up to never fazed young Dan, and he actually used it to spur him on. If his great-uncle could do it, then why couldn't he?

He attended Ellesmere College later on, playing as the first five-eighth for the majority of his time there. He moved to Christchurch Boys' High School for the last year of his education as they had a much better rugby programme, and he wanted to be the best he could be. From that point on, he was always going to be a professional player.

His chance came early, and he signed for Canterbury in 2002. His skills instantly brought him to the attention of the world's best teams, and a year later, the Crusaders came calling. He would spend most of his club career with the Super Rugby legends and would go on to become their record points scorer.

Dan made his New Zealand debut in 2003 at the age of 21. He scored 20 points in a win over Wales and followed it up with a top performance against France in another victory. He was already a fan favourite!

His scoring and determination earned him his spot in the New Zealand squad that flew to Australia for the 2003 World Cup, but he was only used sporadically. New Zealand didn't perform to the best of their abilities, and even though they finished third, questions were asked. On the team's return home, the fans demanded that Dan become a regular part of the first XV.

By 2005, Dan Carter was already considered one of the best fly-halves in the world. In one game that year, he scored two tries, five penalties and four conversions in a 48–18 demolition of the British & Irish Lions. He ended the match with a staggering 33 points, smashing the previous record of 18 (in Lions Tests). His fantastic season was complete when he became the first New Zealander to win the IRB Player of the Year Award.

The following year saw his points tally increasing even more, and he finished the year with 221 points, which was the most ever scored in a single season. Throughout all of this, he led the Crusaders to four consecutive Super Rugby (then Super 12) finals, winning two of them.

He was given a sabbatical* season in 2008–09 so he could join European giants Perpignan on a £30,000-per-game contract. While there, he ruptured his Achilles tendon but still did enough to help the team win the Top 14 title. It was yet another medal for his trophy cabinet!

By the 2010–11 season, Dan Carter and Jonny Wilkinson had built up a friendly rivalry as both players seemed to pass each other on the points leaderboard every other week. Both of them were the record points scorers in Test rugby at several different periods throughout those few years.

Dan played a major part in New Zealand's charge for the 2011 World Cup, but an injury kept him out of the final few games. The team won the competition (their second and Dan's first) in front of their home crowd in what was to become one of the Kiwis' most memorable moments.

He continued this success the following year by becoming the highest-ever points scorer in Super Rugby history when he reached 1,301 points. He was named IRB Player of the Year again!

Dan helped New Zealand to their second consecutive World Cup in 2015 when they beat all before them in England. The final, a 34–17 demolition of arch-rivals Australia, was especially pleasing. Dan kicked two conversions, four penalties and a drop goal. It was a special moment for a special player!

After the World Cup, Dan joined Racing Metro 92, becoming the highest-paid player in the world. While there, he won his third IRB Player of the Year Award and then retired from Test rugby as an international legend! He went out on top, having led his country to their third World Cup.

He found success again at Racing Metro, leading them to the 2016 Top 14 final, where he scored 15 of his team's 29 points as they beat Toulon to clinch the title. He received the Man of the Match award for his standout performance.

A stint at the Kobelco Kobe Steelers in Japan followed as Dan saw out his glittering career. He retired from all forms of rugby in 2021, leaving behind a reputation as possibly the greatest fly-half that ever lived.

Oh, and he once turned down the chance to move to the United States to be a kicker for the New England Patriots in the NFL! Thankfully for rugby, he restricted his career in the sport that he loved and created so many magical moments!

DAVID POCOCK

INTERNATIONAL CAREER

DEBUT	2008
CAPS	78
TRIES	9
POINTS	45

WORLD CUP STATS

DEBUT	2011
TOURNAMENTS	3
TRIES	5
POINTS	25
TITLES	0

BIOGRAPHY

BORN	23 APRIL 1988
NATIONALITY	AUSTRALIAN / ZIMBABWEAN
POSITION(S)	FLANKER, NO. 8
HEIGHT	1.83 M (6 FT 0 IN)
RETIRED	2020

This man wasn't just a world-class rugby player; he also went on to become a senator! He grew up working on his grandparents' farm in terrible conditions and lived in Zimbabwe until his family were forced to flee. David Pocock came through it all to carve out one of the most impressive careers in rugby, and his humanitarian* work has helped millions to live better lives. He is proof that a positive mind and a good heart can overcome anything.

Unlike a lot of the players on this list, David Pocock didn't win many team competitions, but his individual performances made him stand out. He was a loyal player who could have joined one of the European giants and had guaranteed success, but he stayed with the clubs he loved, proving he has always placed loyalty above medals.

Born in Messina, South Africa, and raised in Zimbabwe, David Pocock learned the importance of a hard day's work early on. His grandparents grew vegetables and flowers, which they exported and sold, and he helped out in the mornings before school and in the evenings when his homework was done. The hard work helped to put meat on his bones, and by the time young David had discovered rugby as a kid, he was ready-made for it!

It was at Midlands Christian College that David first

played rugby. He was a natural from the start, and his teachers and coaches encouraged him to pursue it as a career. His progress was halted when civil war broke out in South Africa and white-owned property was taken from its owners and given to South African natives. David and his family were forced to flee, and they moved to Australia.

As soon as they were settled in their new home, David dove into rugby. He practised nonstop, and when he started at Anglican Church Grammar School and met up with future teammate Quade Cooper, things really took off. He and Quade were part of their school team that went unbeaten for a whole season, and their chemistry on the field continued to grow through the years. Following a string of brilliant performances, David was picked for the Australian Schoolboys team. A career in rugby union was inevitable!

His debut came in 2006 when he ran out for the Western Force in their game against the Sharks. He impressed and was soon being talked about as a future Australian flanker. It seemed like it was only a matter of time until he became an international.

In the end, it took just over a year of professional rugby until he was called up to the Wallabies Test side. His debut came against the Barbarians in December of 2008, which was quickly followed by his Test debut against New Zealand. That same year, he captained the under-21s team at the Junior World Championships in Wales.

His breakthrough season was in 2009, and he played in 13 of Australia's 14 Tests that year. He chalked up a couple of Man of the Match awards and scored his first try for the Wallabies against Wales in Cardiff (a 33–12 win). Throughout these matches, David became known for his strength and determination, often playing on through serious injuries such as a dislocated thumb. He has carried this passion and drive into his humanitarian work.

By 2010, he was Australia's starting openside flanker. His performances weren't going unnoticed, and he picked up the John Eales Medal—the highest honour in Australian rugby—at the end of the year. He was also nominated for the IRB Player of the Year award but narrowly lost out to Richie McCaw, so no shame there! Pocock was also a finalist the following year.

A couple of major changes occurred in 2012. His time with the Western Force came to an end when he signed for ACT Brumbies, and he was named Australia's captain while James Horwill was injured. It looked like things were going great, but the following season saw him pick up a nasty injury that required reconstructive knee surgery. By the time he recovered, he'd lost his place in Australia's first XV to Michael Hooper. We'll cover Michael later in the book!

To make matters worse, his recovery only lasted a few weeks, and he damaged his knee again three games into his return. David needed a second operation and more reconstruction surgery on his knee. A lot of people would have given up at this stage, but David Pocock is made of sterner stuff. He knuckled down and completed his rehab, making it back in time for the 2015 Rugby Championship, which Australia won!

The Wallabies went into the 2015 World Cup as one of the favourites, and they came very close. In the end, they lost the final to that fantastic New Zealand team that included Richie McCaw and Dan Carter, among others. Pocock scored a try in the final, but it wasn't enough to stop the All Blacks juggernaut.

A move to Japan's Top League (now called Japan Rugby League One) came in 2016 when David joined the Panasonic Wild Knights. The deal was made with the 2019 World Cup in mind: Pocock would be allowed to return to the Brumbies for the 2018–19 season so he would be ready to play in the tournament.

Australia did well but fell short again, losing to England in the quarterfinals. Pocock retired from international rugby after the tournament, and although he was meant to return to Japan, he decided to finish up with all forms of rugby to concentrate on his charity work.

David Pocock has worked wonders for climate change, same-sex marriage and help for the hearing impaired, among many other things. As well as all this amazing work, he has successfully run for senator and continues to fight for the rights of people, animals and the planet.

A man with the heart of a lion, David Pocock has brought his competitive edge to his professional life outside of rugby, too. He is determined to do the right thing, and there wouldn't be many people on the planet who would want to stand in his way! If his rugby career is anything to go by, he would simply plough right through them if they did!

PAUL O'CONNELL

INTERNATIONAL CAREER

DEBUT	2002
CAPS	115
WINS	69
TRIES	8
POINTS	40

WORLD CUP STATS

DEBUT	2003
TOURNAMENTS	4
CAPS	17
TRIES	0
TITLES	0

International stats include matches for the British & Irish Lions

BIOGRAPHY

BORN	20 OCTOBER 1979
NATIONALITY	IRISH
POSITION(S)	LOCK
HEIGHT	1.98 M (6 FT 6 IN)
RETIRED	2016

Now we have another one of the world's greatest locks and someone who would even give Martin Johnson a run for his money! Paul O'Connell was a beast, both in size and the way he played. At six-foot-six and 111 kilograms (17.5 stone), he was a rock and one of those players who seemed to be able to take his whole team by the scruff of the neck and drag them over the line.

Paul was born in Limerick, Ireland, on 20 October 1979. What makes his journey so amazing is that he didn't play rugby until his late teens! Before then, he tried almost every other sport. Even though he was brilliant at most, he never excelled the way he eventually did with a rugby ball.

Despite his colossal size, Paul actually wanted to be a swimmer in his childhood! He was pretty good, too. During his time at Ardscoil Rís, his teachers encouraged him to try rugby as they saw that rare mix of size and agility in him. As soon as he gave in to their nagging and ran out onto the pitch, he was hooked.

Amazingly, that day came when Paul was already 16! It goes to show that people are literally born to be great at certain things. And Paul was born to play rugby.

Not long after his first proper game of rugby, Paul was playing in the Munster Schools Senior Cup. He performed brilliantly, and he was soon turning out for the Irish under-18s alongside future Ireland star Gordon D'Arcy. When he moved up to the under-21s team, he was joined by another future Ireland player, Donncha O'Callaghan, who was his second-row partner.

After secondary school, Paul studied Computer Engineering at the University of Limerick (UL). He finished three of the four years before leaving to concentrate on his rugby career. It was a decision that proved to be a very good one!

Paul signed for Munster, where he would spend his whole club career. He signed for Toulon at the end of his time at Munster, but injury prevented him from ever making a first-team appearance. While at Munster, he won pretty much everything there was to win.

He made his Munster debut in August 2001 against Edinburgh and quickly followed this up with his first Heineken Cup appearance in a 28–23 win over Castres Olympique. The following year, he reached his first Heineken Cup final, but Munster suffered a heartbreaking defeat to that Martin and Will Johnson-inspired Leicester side.

Paul's first Test match for Ireland came in 2002 at the Six Nations, and he scored a try in a convincing 54–10 thrashing of Wales at Lansdowne Road. Later on, he admitted he had no memory of the try or most of the match, having suffered a concussion early on.

His success with Munster continued to grow, and he helped them win the Celtic League in 2003. Paul's amazing performances at the Six Nations and for Munster earned him a place on the plane to Australia for the 2003 World Cup. He played every game as Ireland reached the quarterfinals, where they were stopped by France.

When an injury to Brian O'Driscoll kept him out of the opening game of the 2004 Six Nations, Paul was asked to captain the side. Ireland lost the game to France, but they still went on to have a great tournament, winning their seventh Triple Crown and their first in 19 years.

After waiting 19 years for a Triple Crown, Ireland won it again in 2006, a feat that included a famous 28–24 victory over England at Twickenham.

Paul O'Connell was one of Munster's best players as they won their first-ever Heineken Cup in 2006, beating Biarritz 23–19 in an electrifying final. They went on to win it again two years later.

In between those fantastic Heineken Cup wins, O'Connell and Ireland continued to grow as a team. When they won another Triple Crown at the 2007 Six Nations (battering England 43–13 along the way), they found themselves going into that year's World Cup as one of the outside favourites. Ireland were expected to make a real impression. They did make an impression, but not in the way they would have hoped. The team played terribly and exited the competition at the pool stage.

Ireland learned their lesson, and a period of success soon followed.

As Munster started to stumble a little in the following years (they were still great, just not as successful), Paul's international career really took off. Ireland won the 2009 Six Nations, claiming their first Grand Slam in 61 years. They won the competition again in 2015 and then retained it the following year.

In his time with Ireland, Paul O'Connell won three Six Nations and was part of one of the best XVs the country has ever produced. With Munster, he was a two-time European champion and won the United Rugby Championship (previously the Celtic League, among many other names) three times. He won the short-lived Celtic Cup once and captained both his club and country on numerous occasions.

An animal on the field and a gentleman off it, Paul O'Connell is someone who represents everything good about rugby as a sport. He was a winner and a leader on the pitch, and he will always be named in any Ireland or Munster greatest-ever XV lists.

DAVID CAMPESE

INTERNATIONAL CAREER

DEBUT	1982
CAPS	101
WINS	67
TRIES	64
POINTS	320

WORLD CUP STATS

DEBUT	1987
TOURNAMENTS	3
CAPS	15
TRIES	10
TITLES	1

BIOGRAPHY

BORN	21 OCTOBER 1962
NATIONALITY	AUSTRALIAN
POSITION(S)	WING, FULLBACK
HEIGHT	1.80 M (5 FT 11 IN)
RETIRED	1996

David Campese was one of the first mavericks in rugby. From his famous "goose-step" shimmy to his post-match interviews, he always entertained and made headlines. He was highly skilled and knew it, and his approach to rugby split opinions between the purists* and the sport's new hip fans. Most of all, he was one of Australia's best and most important players, and he will always be an Aussie idol.

David Campese was born in Queanbeyan, New South Wales, Australia, on 21 October 1962. Although his father was Italian, David grew up in Australia but never lost that Italian flair! Throughout his career, he carried himself with confidence, which helped him become one of the most famous rugby players of his time. Like Jonah Lomu, David's flashy style of play brought rugby to a whole new audience. He was unpredictable and fantastic to watch.

But rugby wasn't always David's first love. He was a fine golfer, and during his time at Queanbeyan High School, he split his time between the fairways and the rugby pitch. As he hit his teens, rugby actually became less of an interest, and for a while, David quit it altogether to concentrate on golf. In the end, his passion for rugby won out, but not before he won the ACT Monaro Schoolboys golf tournament!

At 16, he decided to concentrate solely on rugby, and

his talents exploded. Within a year, he had made his full debut for the Queanbeyan Whites. His rapid rise continued when he played for the Australia under-21s throughout their tour of New Zealand, and he made his debut against the All Blacks. David did so well that he was offered a trial for the upcoming Aussie tour of Britain and Ireland.

His Test debut for Australia came in 1982 when they toured New Zealand again, scoring a try in each of his first two matches. He followed this up by racking up four tries in one game as the Wallabies demolished the USA. And it didn't stop there. During a tour of Britain and Ireland, David Campese was part of the Aussie team that beat all four home nations for the first time ever.

Campese started out on the wing, but he was soon moved to fullback and spent his career moving between both positions. It was at fullback that he would receive praise from some fans and criticism from others. When playing in a supposedly defensive position, he added a new, stylish form of attack. But his risk-taking often caused havoc at the back when his maverick ways backfired. For the younger fans, Campese was a revolutionary*. The older fans thought he was a liability*.

David was called up to the Australian team for the first-ever Rugby World Cup in 1987 but struggled with injuries throughout. The Aussies lost in the semifinals to France and then lost a tight third-place playoff to Wales. The tournament was seen as a disaster for both Campese and the Australia squad as a whole, but only because they had been unfairly expected to win it without a problem by some fans and pundits*.

Even though they lost, the game against France was a classic. Often thought of as one of the greatest World Cup matches ever, Campese and his teammates battled hard against a well-drilled French side. David scored a brilliant try six minutes into the game, which broke a then-54-year-old record: It was his 25th test try! In the end, France won 30–24, but the game remains one of Campese's favourites despite the result. To him, it was how rugby should be played. Fast-paced, competitive and attacking.

The injuries picked up before and during the tournament continued to hound him for the next couple of years. He returned to play in a two-Test series against England in 1988, but his risk-taking and flamboyant* style was starting to grate on some of his coaches. Again, the crowd loved him for it, but some of the purists complained.

It came to a head in a series match against the Lions in 1989 when his mistake led to a deciding try. Several pundits and even his own coach had something to say about it, and none of it was nice. The criticism hurt David, who felt that he took those risks to gain an advantage for his team, not to lose games.

And his risks often did benefit his team. David's "miracle pass" to Tim Horan against New Zealand at the 1991 World Cup is still seen as one of the most genius moments ever on a rugby pitch. It helped the Wallabies to a famous victory, and they went on to win their first World Cup. Campese scored the most tries at the tournament (six) and claimed the World Player of the Year award at the end of the campaign. Even his critics had to applaud him now.

He played in his third World Cup four years later, which South Africa won. That was also the tournament when Jonah Lomu burst onto the scene, scoring seven tries! Australia went out to England in the quarterfinals, and the team went home feeling a little deflated.

The following year saw Campese reach 100 Test caps in a game against Italy in Padova, which was fitting, as he had played for the local club. His next cap was his last, and it came against Wales in Cardiff. The fans knew it would be his final game, and over 70,000 Welsh supporters showed up to give him a standing ovation.

Sadly for David, his retirement in 1996 came just as rugby was becoming a professional sport. Now, players were earning more, and the flamboyant guys were signing the best contracts. It's fair to say that David would have easily become one of the highest-paid players in the world. Every club would have been fighting for his signature because he wasn't just a winner; he put bums on seats*!

Since his playing days, David has become a very successful media personality, and he is famed for taking every opportunity to criticise the England team! It's all in good fun, and anyone who knows him would admit that he loves nothing more than stirring up a bit of controversy. He was awarded the Order of Australia in 2002, but it is his skills with a rugby ball that he'll always be remembered for. Without David Campese, rugby would be light years behind where it is now!

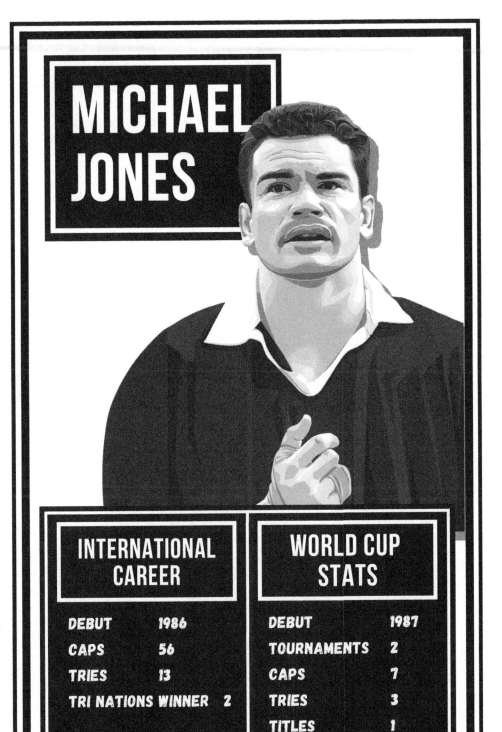

MICHAEL JONES

INTERNATIONAL CAREER

DEBUT	1986
CAPS	56
TRIES	13
TRI NATIONS WINNER	2

WORLD CUP STATS

DEBUT	1987
TOURNAMENTS	2
CAPS	7
TRIES	3
TITLES	1

BIOGRAPHY

BORN	**8 APRIL 1965**
NATIONALITY	**NEW ZEALANDER**
POSITION(S)	**FLANKER, NUMBER EIGHT**
HEIGHT	**1.85 M (6 FT 1 IN)**
RETIRED	**1999**

Sometimes, things are bigger than sports. We fans can often get carried away when the passion for our team takes over, and we forget that the players have other things going on in their lives. They deal with all of the stuff we do—good and bad—but we sometimes see them as superheroes who only appear when we see them on the field, in the ring or on the court.

One such player who reminds us of this is Michael Jones. He is a man who refused to change his beliefs no matter how much pressure was put on him. He was and is a strict Christian, which means he can't work on Sundays. Because of this, he missed many important games and even a World Cup. Still, he never gave in, and he always put his faith first.

We think there is a lesson there for all of us: If you believe in something good, then never let anyone tell you differently.

Born in Auckland, New Zealand, on 8 April 1965, Michael grew up in the suburb of Te Atatū South. It wasn't a very wealthy area, yet he stayed loyal to the city of his birth his whole provincial career. In fact, it was this challenging upbringing that made him the man he is today, and he continues to do endless charity work for underprivileged communities. So much so that he was knighted in 2017!

Michael attended several schools in his youth, and he always impressed his teachers and coaches. At the age of 10, he was spotted playing in a match that was full of 15- and 16-year-olds. According to legend, he not only competed with the older kids but bossed the game, slamming into tackles and scoring for fun. From then on, he only ever played competitive youth rugby with boys several years older than him.

By the time he reached Henderson High School, he was a minor Auckland celebrity. Before he started at Henderson, the school team was just average. Auckland Grammar and Kelston Boys' High had always dominated, but they suddenly found themselves behind Henderson. Michael almost single-handedly won championships for his team.

Surprisingly, he didn't make his provincial debut until he was 20. His coaches at the time held him back, knowing he would be a pro in good time. They wanted him fully ready... and it worked. Michael scored a hat trick on his debut against South Canterbury!

One strange fact about Michael Jones is that he made his international debut for Western Samoa and not New Zealand. His mother was from there, and Samoa tried to tempt Michael over to their side. He liked it with the Samoans, but his heart was always with the All Blacks, and his debut came at the 1987 World Cup!

The firsts didn't stop there! Not only was it the first-ever World Cup in history and Jones's first-ever game for New Zealand, but he scored the first-ever try at any World Cup and went on to win New Zealand's first-ever World Cup trophy! Phew, that was a lot of "first-evers"!

Michael played in most of the games, including the final, but soon after the World Cup, his injuries started. They would plague him for the rest of his career, starting with a horrible knee injury in 1989. He had a serious jaw break a few years later and then an even more serious knee injury a few years after that. There were lots of little niggly injuries in between, which meant that throughout his Kiwi career, Jones only managed to play in 55 of New Zealand's 90 games over that period.

Of course, he also missed games due to his religious beliefs, which included three of the games that fell on Sundays at the 1991 World Cup. He wasn't even called up to the squad for the 1995 World Cup after the selectors saw that the quarter and semifinals fell on Sundays.

When asked how he could have such strong religious beliefs, seeing as he smashed into people for a living, he is said to have quoted the Bible verse about being better to give than to receive.

Michael Jones is known as much for his provincial career as he is for his international career. He played for Auckland between 1985 and 1999, winning 10 National Provincial Championships. Four of these came in a row during what is now known as one of the most dominant periods by any team in rugby.

Auckland and Jones defended the Ranfurly Shield* an astonishing 61 times in a row during this period! Add to this the first- and second-ever Super 12 (now Super Rugby) titles, and you have one stuffed trophy cabinet!

Surprisingly, Jones's injuries actually lessened as he got older, and he played some of his best rugby during his golden years. He retired from all forms of rugby in 1999, and apart from a three-year stint coaching Samoa, he now concentrates on his charity work.

Michael Jones is a role model. He is the type of person we should all aspire to be, and not just because of what he did on a rugby pitch. If we all carry ourselves with the same dignity, then good things will happen. It's just a matter of being kind to others and sticking to our beliefs!

SCHALK BURGER

INTERNATIONAL CAREER

DEBUT	2003
CAPS	86
WINS	57
TRIES	16
POINTS	80

WORLD CUP STATS

DEBUT	2003
TOURNAMENTS	4
CAPS	20
TRIES	4
TITLES	1

BIOGRAPHY

BORN	13 APRIL 1983
NATIONALITY	SOUTH AFRICAN
POSITION(S)	LOOSE-FORWARD
HEIGHT	1.93 M (6 FT 4 IN)
RETIRED	2019

Some rugby fans would describe Schalk Burger as aggressive, while others would call him competitive. Maybe he was a bit of both when he stepped out onto the pitch, but rugby is an aggressive and competitive sport. For players like Schalk, yellow cards and hard tackles are part of the game. They are what make rugby the sport we love.

Apart from his powerful way of playing, Schalk Burger was also one of the best flankers the game has ever seen. At six-foot-four and 251 pounds (nearly 18 stone), he was an intimidating figure. But he could play. He was so much more than a powerhouse. But his aggressive style did bring problems, and not just for his opponents. Constantly smashing into opponents meant that he suffered from injuries throughout his career.

Schalk Burger was born into a rugby-obsessed family in Port Elizabeth, South Africa, on 13 April 1983. His father (also called Schalk Burger) was a South African international, and he helped shape his son into one of the Springboks' greatest players. When he started school at Paarl Gimnasium, young Schalk was a classmate of future South Africa captain Jean de Villiers. He was surrounded by the sport!

Following his time at Paarl Gimnasium, Schalk briefly attended Stellenbosch University before leaving to pursue his rugby career.

It wasn't long before he was called up to the South African under-21 side that competed at the 2002 World Cup, which was won by New Zealand. He began his provincial career that year, too, playing his first games for the Western Province before signing for the Stormers in the Super 12 (now Super Rugby). After just a few games for the Springboks' under-21s, he was named captain.

His Test career began at the 2003 Rugby World Cup, making his debut against Georgia. He performed well, but South Africa went out in the quarterfinals to New Zealand. Schalk and the Springboks would return in 2007 to lift the title, but we'll come to that!

Before that could happen, South African rugby needed a new look. It came with the appointment of Jake White, who wanted to build the team around young, competitive, energetic players like Schalk. His new system had an instant impact, and South Africa won the 2004 Tri Nations, their first since 1998.

Just as things were looking up, Schalk started to suffer from the injuries that would affect his whole career. His lack of play time had such an effect that he lost his place in the South Africa first XV for a while. He trained hard and won it back in time for the 2006 Tri Nations, but his fitness didn't last. A serious neck injury against Scotland kept him out for six months, and it was so bad that his doctors suggested he never play again.

His rehab was tough, but Schalk managed to slowly

regain fitness and, more importantly, strengthen his neck. He returned to first-team action for the Stormers in January 2007, playing 55 minutes before being subbed off for protection. His coaches must have been tempted to rush him back into action, as the Stormers really needed him at that moment. The 2007 Super 14 season had started terribly without their star flanker, proving his worth more than ever.

On the international stage, things were looking up again. The 2007 World Cup in France was fast approaching, and Jake White had built a team the fans believed could go all the way. As we saw earlier in the chapter, the fans were right! The Springboks beat the holders England in the final, restricting them to just two penalties from Jonny Wilkinson in a 15–6 victory.

It was South Africa's second World Cup and Schalk Burger's first, and a moment that he would remember forever. But it wasn't all perfect for him, and he nearly missed the majority of the tournament after a bad high tackle in the opening game against Samoa. Schalk received a four-game ban, which was reduced to a two-game ban on appeal. He returned in time for the knockout phase, and the rest is history!

The 2011 World Cup was less successful, with South Africa going out in the quarterfinals. It was an impressive year for Schalk personally, and he picked up the SARU Rugby Player of the Year award for the second time in his career, becoming one of only two South African players to win it twice.

His run of injuries soon started to pile up. He was diagnosed with spinal meningitis in 2014 but somehow managed to recover in time for the 2015 World Cup. In fact, he was awarded the Comeback of the Year award for his efforts, and he managed to play all seven of the Springboks games before they went out in the semis in a tightly fought classic against eventual winners New Zealand.

Schalk retired from Test rugby following South Africa's victory over Argentina in the third-place playoff, bringing an end to his wonderful international career.

He joined Saracens in 2016 after a 12-year stint with the Stormers. He played for the North London club for three highly successful years, where he won the European Champions Cup twice. Following the 2019 final, Schalk retired from all forms of rugby.

In August 2012, Schalk Burger and his wife Michele announced the birth of their son, Schalk Jnr. Could we one day see a third-generation Burger playing for South Africa? Who knows, but if the kid is anything like his father and grandfather, we think it's safe to say there is a very good chance!

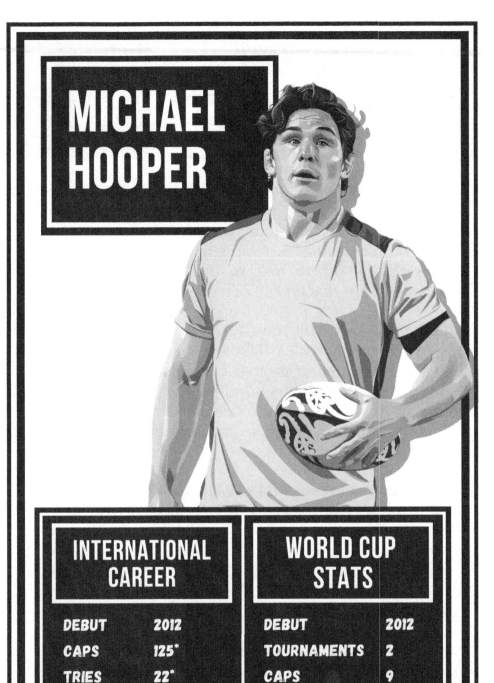

MICHAEL HOOPER

INTERNATIONAL CAREER

DEBUT	2012
CAPS	125*
TRIES	22*
POINTS	110*

WORLD CUP STATS

DEBUT	2012
TOURNAMENTS	2
CAPS	9
TRIES	3
TITLES	0

BIOGRAPHY

BORN	29 OCTOBER 1991
NATIONALITY	AUSTRALIAN
POSITION(S)	FLANKER
HEIGHT	1.82 M (6 FT 0 IN)
RETIRED	STILL PLAYING

Now, we have one of the few players on this list who are still playing at the time of this book being written. For any sportsperson to be considered a legend while they're still playing takes something special. They have to really be superb to earn that right, and Michael Hooper is just that type of player.

Although he's still not finished playing, Michael Hooper already has 125 Test appearances for Australia, making him one of the most capped players in their history. But who knows how high that number will go! His staying power* is a reflection of his fitness, skill and the amount of work he puts in both on and off the pitch.

Born on 29 October 1991 in Manly, New South Wales, Michael grew up loving sports. He played football for the famous Manly Roos kids' team, who have produced players such as George Smith. All of Michael's youth rugby was played at the highest level. He was exceptional from the moment he first picked up a ball.

It seemed natural that he would slot straight into the Australian youth teams, and he did, captaining the under-20s at the 2011 IRB Junior World Championships. He dominated, being named International Player of the Tournament at the end. By now, every major club in the world wanted to sign him.

But the Brumbies had already won his signature, and he made his debut at the age of 19. In an amazing twist, his debut came when he was subbed on for George Smith, the kid who had graduated from the Manly Roos a decade before him!

He didn't have to wait long for his Test debut, coming off the bench in a match against Scotland in June 2012. Later that year, a knee injury to David Pocock (the guy we covered earlier in the book!) meant that Michael started every Test game for the remainder of that season. As we know, the friendly competition between Pocock and Hooper drove both players to their best.

His breakthrough year continued at club level when he was named Best Forward and Rookie of the Year after several standout performances for the Brumbies. Already known as one of the most promising players in the world, it was only a matter of time until the big boys came calling. The New South Wales Waratahs won the race for his signature, and he signed for them in 2013. It would prove a long and successful partnership!

When David Pocock picked up another season-ending injury, Michael stepped in to replace him once more. Again, he played every Test match and performed brilliantly throughout the year, winning the Wallabies Player of the Year award. And Michael wasn't just a machine for Australia. He played every game of the Waratahs Super Rugby campaign that year, and he was named their best player at the end of the season.

He was named his club's captain in the Waratahs' game against the Queensland Reds in March 2014, meaning he was still 22 when given this honour! The Waratahs won the match 32–5, and he followed this up with another win the next time he captained them, a 33–32 defeat of the Crusaders.

That same year, another injury struck Pocock down, and once again, Michael stepped in as flanker. He was also named Australia's vice-captain and went on to play as captain later that year when he replaced the injured Stephen Moore. Michael Hooper was only 23 years and 233 days old, making him the youngest captain of the Wallabies since 1961!

By 2015, Michael's form for club and country was so good that he forced Pocock into the number 8 position when the latter* returned from injury. This was something unthinkable a couple of years before, given how important a player Pocock had always been for the team. Michael kept his spot for the 2015 World Cup, leading Australia to the final, which they lost to rivals New Zealand.

Two years later, he was named Australia's permanent captain, a role he maintained up until 2022. Known for his aggressive style of play and passion, Michael continues to perform at the highest level for the Waratahs and Australia. His record of nine yellow cards in Test rugby is a joint one, but it only proves how determined he is to win the ball back for his side.

He played his 100th Test match for Australia in 2020, becoming the youngest player in history to do so. The record was later broken by George North, but it makes the accomplishment no less remarkable. And anyway, Michael wasn't finished there. The following year, he surpassed George Gregan's record for most caps as Australia's captain!

Still in his early thirties, Michael Hooper continues to astound fans around the world. Given his fitness and the way he looks after his body, who knows how many more star performances he will put in before he hangs up his boots! Most players need to finish their careers before they are considered a legend; Michael Hooper already is one!

SERGE BLANCO

INTERNATIONAL CAREER

DEBUT	1980
CAPS	93
TRIES	38
POINTS	233
GRAND SLAMS	2

WORLD CUP STATS

DEBUT	1987
TOURNAMENTS	2
TRIES	2
TITLES	0
RUNNERS-UP	1

BIOGRAPHY

BORN	31 AUGUST 1958
NATIONALITY	FRENCH / VENEZUELAN
POSITION(S)	FULLBACK, WING
HEIGHT	1.83 M (6 FT 0 IN)
RETIRED	1992

Like David Campese, Serge Blanco was a player who revelled in turning defence into attack. And again, like Campese, he played a lot of his early career as a winger. So, by the time he moved back into a defensive position, he was already a fantastic attacking threat. He played 93 times for France, a record at the time, and is considered by most to be their greatest player.

Serge was actually born in Venezuela, but his parents moved to France when he was very young. His father was Venezuelan, and his mother Basque, but Serge always felt French inside. As far back as he could remember, he lived and went to school in France and spoke French. All his friends were French. It was only natural that he would want to play for the national team when he grew up.

And what a place he grew up in! Biarritz is beautiful, and Serge loved it there. Once he was old enough to play pro rugby, Biarritz was the team he chose, and he stayed there his whole career. But it was with France where he really made his name, spending most of his years with the national team playing alongside fellow all-time legends Jean-Pierre Rives and Philippe Sella.

He played for France at the first World Cup in 1987, and it was here that he made his permanent mark on rugby. France played brilliantly, making it all the way to the final, but lost to New Zealand. Still, there were some truly memorable matches along the way.

Their first game against Scotland was a classic, with Blanco scoring a try, a conversion and two penalties. He scored another try—one of the greatest of all time —in a back-and-forth battle with Australia. This was the game that David Campese claimed was one of the greatest matches he ever played in, and he wasn't wrong! France came out 30–24 winners and booked their place in the final.

The Kiwis were a step too far for France, but Blanco was one of the top performers at the tournament. His best moment was that try against Australia. Blanco ran the length of the field, evading tackles and leaving the Aussie team in his wake before grounding the ball, completing a World Cup moment that will live on forever.

His time with Biarritz wasn't nearly as successful. They were far from one of the biggest teams in the world, and people often questioned Serge's decision to stay with them. He could have played for any team in the world and won endless trophies, but he loved Biarritz, and he couldn't see himself pulling on any other jersey.

Serge played for Biarritz for 18 years, and the closest they came to major silverware was in his final season! After a long battle for the French Championship (now the Top 14), Biarritz and Serge stumbled at the final hurdle, finishing second. It would have been a Hollywood moment if Serge had led such a small club to their first-ever championship in his last season, but it just wasn't to be.

By the 1991 World Cup (jointly hosted by England, Wales, Scotland, France and Ireland), Serge was captain of his country. He led them into the tournament as one of the favourites, but they stumbled at the quarterfinal stage. France started well, dominating their pool with wins over Romania, Canada and Fiji. A quarterfinal loss against England ended the French dreams, and Serge retired from international rugby after the tournament.

He played on for Biarritz in that heartbreaking last season before retiring from all forms of rugby.

Off the field, Serge Blanco is an extremely successful businessman. He owns a clothing company and several luxury hotels, and he served on the board of his beloved Biarritz. In his time as the president of Biarritz, he finally saw his hometown club win the French Championship. They did it twice, in 2002 and 2006. They also just missed out on the Heineken Cup in 2006 and 2010, losing the final both times.

Serge Blanco was on the list of the first players ever inducted into the International Hall of Fame in 1997, and he was inducted into the IRB Hall of Fame in 2011. His skill as an attacking fullback has inspired generations of flamboyant players in the years that followed his retirement. Much like David Campese and several others on this list, Serge Blanco changed the way the sport of rugby is played.

Some players are legends due to their massive trophy cabinet, and others because of what they did for the game. Serge Blanco falls into the second category. A true trailblazer and one of those exceptional players who gets fans up off their seats. A legend of the game.

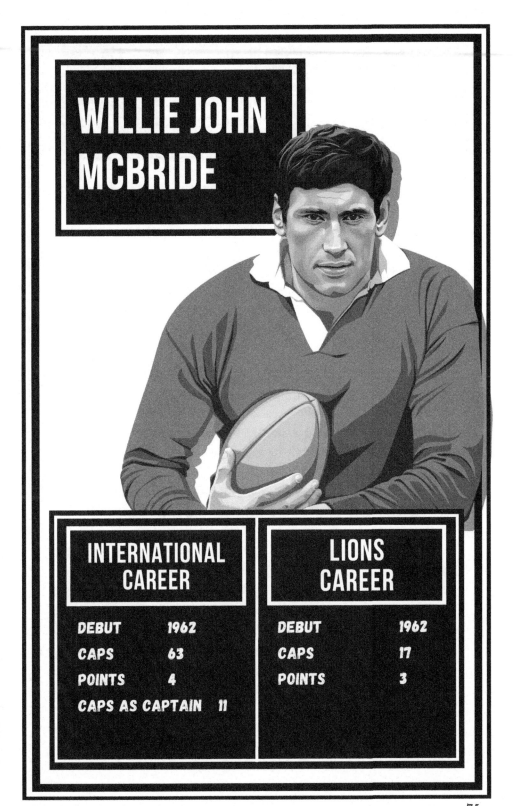

WILLIE JOHN MCBRIDE

INTERNATIONAL CAREER

DEBUT	1962
CAPS	63
POINTS	4
CAPS AS CAPTAIN	11

LIONS CAREER

DEBUT	1962
CAPS	17
POINTS	3

75

BIOGRAPHY

BORN	**6 JUNE 1940**
NATIONALITY	**NORTHERN IRISH**
POSITION(S)	**LOCK**
HEIGHT	**1.92 M (6 FT 3 IN)**
RETIRED	**1975**

Although an Irish rugby legend, Willie John McBride was also famed for his fantastic British & Irish Lions career. In his five tours with the Lions, they recorded some of their finest results, and Willie was a huge part of that. What's amazing is that he didn't even try the sport until he was nearly an adult! A gentle giant off the field, Willie John McBride was an absolute animal on it!

Willie was born in Toomebridge, County Antrim, on 6 June 1940, growing up on his family's farm. Life was tough, and the McBrides often struggled to pay the bills. When his father died, Willie was just 4, and he quickly had to learn how to work the land. It was because of this that the young Willie never got a chance to play rugby. He didn't get to play any sports. He had to work every day before and after school.

In fact, Willie was 17 when he first picked up a rugby ball, but he didn't need much of an introduction. Already a tall lad, he was also stocky and fit due to his hard work on the farm throughout his childhood. His school's rugby team were decent, but they drastically improved once Willie joined. At 17, his teammates must have thought it too late for a player to start a new sport, but they were soon convinced.

Willie left school and joined Ballymena RFC. There wasn't much of a league in Ireland in the fifties and sixties, so most of Willie's magical moments would come with the Irish national team and the Lions. Even with his successful career growing on the pitch, he continued to tend to his family's farm in between matches. It was a tough life, but Willie John McBride is a tough man!

Five years after playing his first-ever rugby match, Willie made his Ireland debut in February 1962 in a Test match against England at Twickenham. Later that year, he was selected for the Lions tour of South Africa. It was a rapid rise.

Back in Willie's era, rugby wasn't the global sport it is now. Most of the home nations only really played each other. Travelling to the southern hemisphere or having those teams come to Britain and Ireland was a big deal. It was glamorous. So, when Ireland played the mighty South Africa in 1965, it was a big deal. And they didn't just play them; the Irish won! It was the first time they'd ever beaten the Springboks.

They followed this up later in the year by beating Australia in Sydney. It was the first time any of the home nations had beaten the Wallabies on their own patch.

Willie toured Australia again in 1966, this time with the Lions. Two years later, they toured New Zealand. For the poor kid from a farm in Toomebridge, it was an amazing time. He never would have dreamed of such things as he worked the land as a child before traipsing off to school!

And those tours weren't even the height of his Lions

career. Those two moments came in 1971 and 1974. The first of these, a tour of New Zealand, was unbelievable for a lot of reasons. For one thing, the newspapers had already claimed that Willie was too old for top Test rugby. Still, he was named pack leader and drove the Lions to a massive series win over the Kiwis.

Even more impressively, he was selected again in 1974 for that tour of South Africa. If the press thought he was over the hill in 1971, they really thought he was too old by '74. Again, Willie was selected as pack leader, and once more, he led the team to a series win. It was the first time the Lions had won a Test series in South Africa, and it didn't come easy. It is now known as the invincible series, as the Lions won 3-0.

The three games against the Springboks are often remembered as the most brutal series of matches in the history of rugby. Headbutts, kicks and fistfights repeatedly broke out all over the pitch. At half-time in the opening match, the Lions were shocked by the tactics of the South Africans. They'd never seen such aggression on a pitch. McBride took control of the team talk and told his teammates that they had to fight fire with fire. He ordered them to follow a "one in, all in" policy.

This meant that if one Lions player got hit off the ball, the whole team hit whatever South African player was closest to them! As nasty as the tactic was, it worked! It is considered one of the greatest moments in Lions history and Willie's career.

A year later, Willie played his final home game for

Ireland at Lansdowne Road. A massive crowd turned out to see him play against France, and he treated them to a spectacle, scoring his only try in an Irish shirt! His last-ever game came soon after against Wales in Cardiff. Again, a huge crowd turned up to show their support. It was yet another magical moment in the life of Willie John McBride.

Since his retirement, he has coached the Irish and Lions teams at different times. He was one of the original inductees into the Rugby Hall of Fame in 1997, and he has regularly been brought in to give inspirational speeches before Lions games through the years. We think it's safe to say that the mere sight of a legend like Willie in the dressing room would be enough to motivate any team.

One of his biggest honours came in 2004 when he was named Rugby Personality of the Century. It doesn't get much better than that!

Away from the sport, Willie does a lot of charity work. He is one of the main supporters of the charity organisation, the Wooden Spoon Society*, and was awarded a CBE* in 2019. It was his massive heart that helped him become one of the best players ever, and it has also driven him to do everything he can for those less fortunate.

Willie John McBride is a gentleman and a legend of the game. A true hero.

RICHIE MCCAW

INTERNATIONAL CAREER

DEBUT	2001
CAPS	148
WINS	131
TRIES	27
POINTS	135

WORLD CUP STATS

DEBUT	2003
TOURNAMENTS	4
CAPS	22
TRIES	3
TITLES	2

BIOGRAPHY

BORN	31 DECEMBER 1980
NATIONALITY	NEW ZEALANDER
POSITION(S)	FLANKER, NUMBER 8
HEIGHT	1.87 M (6 FT 2 IN)
RETIRED	2015

Here we have another New Zealander and the first All Black to reach 100 caps for his country. Winning one cap for a team as strong as New Zealand is an achievement. Playing 148 times for them is nothing short of genius.

Richard Hugh McCaw was born on New Year's Eve, 1980, in Oamaru, New Zealand. He grew up on his family's farm and worked hard from an early age. The physical labour and exercise helped fill him out. Years later, when he was in his prime, Richie McCaw was six-foot-two and 107 kilograms (16 stone 12 pounds). Farm work had helped him to grow into a giant of a player.

He wasn't the only one in his family who excelled in sports growing up. His sister Joanna was a brilliant netball player who represented New Zealand at the highest level.

As a kid, Richie only played rugby for fun in the fields around his family's farm. But in 1994, when he started at the Otago Boys' High School (a secondary school in Dunedin), things really took off. Richie thrived at boarding school. He was used to getting up early, working hard and following the rules, so it came naturally to him.

Otago also had a top rugby programme, and Richie's talents were quickly spotted by his coaches. By his final year, he was head boy and one of the best players in a team that was stacked with future rugby stars. In a final against Rotorua Boys' High School in 1998, between them, the two teams included players such as Angus MacDonald, Sam Harding, Hale T-Pole and Richie McCaw!

After high school, Richie earned a place at the University of Otago. He studied for a Bachelor of Agricultural Science degree as his rugby career continued to blossom. He played for the New Zealand under-19s in 1999 at the World Championships in Wales and helped them win the trophy. He knew then that a career in professional rugby wasn't just a dream anymore.

The following year saw three more debuts. The New Zealand under-21s and Canterbury came first. His Canterbury start was against North Harbour in the National Provincial Championship (NPC). This was soon followed by his first Super Rugby appearance when he stepped out for the Crusaders.

He was soon captain of the under-21s, and his full debut came against Ireland at Lansdowne Road on 17 November 2001. The All Blacks won 40–29, and Richie McCaw impressed. One of his crunching tackles led to the ball being picked up by Jonah Lomu, who ran it to the line for a try. Richie ended the game with the Man of the Match award.

By 2003, Richie was one of the most important players on the Canterbury, Crusaders and New Zealand teams. He won the Super Rugby final in 2002 but lost it at the same stage the following year. He finished the season being voted International Newcomer of the Year.

He played at the 2003 World Cup, where New Zealand lost to arch-rivals Australia in the semifinals. It was devastating for him, but he was still only 22. Richie McCaw had plenty of time to win a World Cup. And he did... twice!

If Richie's rise hadn't already been rapid, he was also named captain of New Zealand for their game against Wales in 2004. Regular captain Tana Umaga was injured, and Richie stepped in and performed brilliantly. He was only 23.

As the 2007 World Cup rolled around, Richie and his teammates felt they were ready to bring it home. They were wrong. The whole tournament was a disaster as the Kiwis were dumped out in the quarterfinals by France. New Zealand were starting to get the reputation of a big team that folds under pressure.

It seemed like things would be even worse for Richie as the 2011 World Cup approached. He fractured his foot, and to make matters worse, one of the screws used to hold the bones in place came loose as the tournament began. Richie somehow played on, captaining his team to the final, where they played France at Eden Park in Auckland.

In front of his home fans, Richie helped New Zealand to a hard-fought 9–8 win. They had won the World Cup!

The 2015 World Cup final was the complete opposite of the drab affair in 2011. With a packed Twickenham crowd watching, New Zealand trounced their old enemy, Australia, 34–17. Richie McCaw had his second World Cup in the bag! In his final game for New Zealand, Richie led the team to one of their greatest-ever moments, and at Twickenham, too—the home of rugby!

He retired after the 2015 World Cup with 148 caps for his country, winning 131 of them, which is a world record. He won 10 Tri-Nations and two World Cups, and he was New Zealand Player of the Year four times.

A true legend and an absolute monster of a player. There aren't many like Richie McCaw.

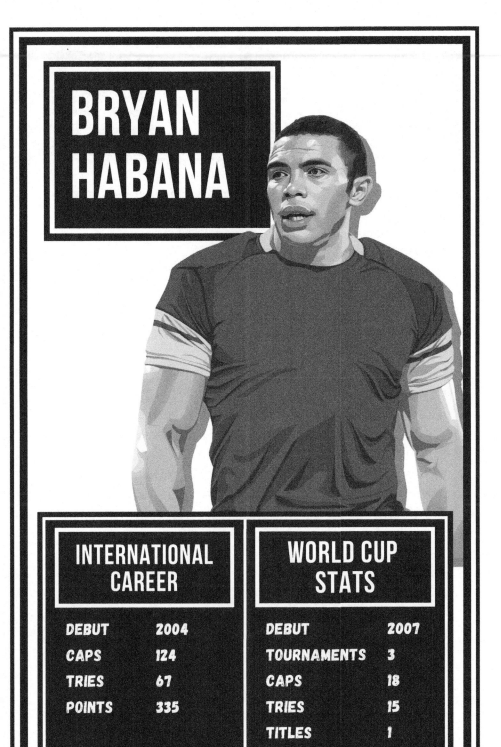

BRYAN HABANA

INTERNATIONAL CAREER

DEBUT	2004
CAPS	124
TRIES	67
POINTS	335

WORLD CUP STATS

DEBUT	2007
TOURNAMENTS	3
CAPS	18
TRIES	15
TITLES	1

BIOGRAPHY

BORN	12 JUNE 1983
NATIONALITY	SOUTH AFRICAN
POSITION(S)	WING / OUTSIDE CENTRE
HEIGHT	1.80 M (5 FT 11 IN)
RETIRED	2018

We have seen some players with stacked trophy cabinets, but not many in history have cleaned up in the way Bryan Habana did during his glittering career. Lightening quick and the record-scorer in Tier One rugby*, he completed a clean sweep of trophies at both international and club levels. His eight tries at the 2007 World Cup equalled Jonah Lomu's record, and he equalled the great man again in 2015 for total World Cup tries!

Bryan Gary Habana was born in Johannesburg on 12 June 1983. His parents clearly saw a future in sports for their son, as his first and middle names were chosen in honour of Bryan Robson and Gary Bailey of Manchester United. Bryan didn't end up being a professional footballer like Robson and Bailey, but he did become one of the greatest wingers in the history of rugby, so not a bad result!

As a kid, Bryan attended the King Edward VII School in Johannesburg, where he played rugby, among many other sports. He was one of the quickest in his class, yet he spent most of his time at outside centre and scrum half. It was when he was moved to the wing that things really took off.

By the time he'd started at Rand Afrikaans University (now the University of Johannesburg), he was a full-fledged winger. He played in the South African Sevens side at the World Seven Series for the 2003–2004 season, impressing and earning a spot on the Golden Lions team who were playing in that year's Currie Cup. His remarkable 2004 continued when he made his Test debut against England at Twickenham in November, and he came off the bench to score a try with his first touch. He was just 21!

He was given a starting spot in South Africa's next game against Scotland at Murrayfield Stadium. He scored two tries and performed brilliantly. When he was picked in the starting XV for the following game against Argentina, it was generally accepted that he was already one of the Springboks' leading players.

At the end of the season, Habana was voted South Africa's most promising player.

The next step up for Bryan was at club level. The Blue Bulls came calling, signing him from the Golden Lions after one season. He was thrown straight into their starting XV for the 2005 Super 12 season. He continued his fine form by being selected for the South Africa squad for that year's Tri Nations, and he played his first game at that level against Australia at the Loftus Versfeld Stadium, the home of his new club!

South Africa won 22–16 and then went on to beat the mighty Kiwis in the next game. In their return game against Australia in Perth, South Africa won again, this time with Habana scoring two tries. Unfortunately, they lost their final match—a tight 27–31 defeat to New Zealand, meaning they just lost out on the Tri Nations trophy. Still, Habana was the tournament's star and top scorer, and now the world knew what he was about.

A near-perfect year for Bryan ended with heartbreak. The Blue Bulls reached the Currie Cup final but suffered a shock loss to underdogs, the Free State Cheetahs. Habana would have to wait to get his hands on the Currie Cup, but his time would come!

Habana was flourishing in the South African side, being transformed by head coach Jake White. Alongside other young stars such as Schalk Burger and Percy Montgomery (he is coming up!), the team was in the process of building toward the 2007 World Cup. As we've seen in earlier chapters, Jake White's side prevailed, and Habana was a massive part of that!

On a lighter note, Bryan took part in a foot race against a cheetah in 2007. Yep, an actual cheetah! It was done for charity, as Bryan wanted to raise money and awareness. Cheetahs are an endangered species, and Bryan has always had a big heart, so he did all he could to help. To make things fair, Bryan was given a 50-metre head start. The race was too close to call, with both man and animal crossing the line at the same time!

A cracker of a final in the Super 14 saw Bryan nearly sent off for a high tackle early on. He escaped a red card and then went on to score a wonder try in the final minute. Derick Hougaard kicked a simple conversion, and the Blue Bulls won the game 20–19 to lift the trophy. It was one of many in Bryan Habana's career.

His biggest win was just around the corner. It came that October when the Springboks lifted the 2007 World Cup. It was the tournament where Habana scored his record-equalling eight tries, including four in the opening game against Samoa. He scored a couple more against the USA and then two against Argentina in the semifinal. His World Cup winners medal is one of his prized possessions!

Bryan Habana went on to win the IRB Player of the Year, which came as a surprise to nobody.

He seemed to suffer a little from the highs of 2007, and the following year was a bit of a bust. Almost impossibly, he only managed two tries for South Africa all year, and the team also performed badly in that season's Tri Nations. But Habana's slump didn't last. He was back to his sublime best in 2009!

Apart from scoring a staggering number of tries that year, he helped South Africa to the Tri Nations and the Blue Bulls to the Super 14 trophy. He also won the Currie Cup for good measure! He was a major part of the Springboks side that beat the British & Irish Lions during their tour of South Africa. He was back to winning ways, and he had no intention of stopping!

After a three-year period with the Stormers, Habana moved to Europe in 2013, linking up with Jonny Wilkinson and an array of other stars at Toulon. They won the 2014 Heineken Cup and Super 14 and then retained their European title the following year.

The 2015 World Cup saw him equal Lomu's all-time record for tries, including a hat trick against America. But South Africa lost to New Zealand in the semis, meaning Habana had missed his last chance to win a second World Cup. Still, he was made vice-captain that season and scored his record 67th try.

Bryan Habana retired from all forms of rugby in 2018, leaving behind a legacy as one of the most explosive players ever to play the game. He started the Bryan Habana Foundation in 2015, a charity organisation that helps underprivileged kids make the most of themselves. His charity work stretches beyond his foundation, and he has helped deliver food to people in need, fight gender discrimination and promote a better South Africa for the next generation.

A true superhero, both on and off the field!

GAVIN HASTINGS

INTERNATIONAL CAREER

DEBUT	1986
CAPS	67
TRIES	18
POINTS	733
CAPS AS CAPTAIN	20

WORLD CUP STATS

DEBUT	1987
TOURNAMENTS	3
TRIES	8
POINTS	227
TITLES	0

International stats include matches for the British & Irish Lions

BIOGRAPHY

BORN	3 JANUARY 1962
NATIONALITY	SCOTTISH
POSITION(S)	FULLBACK
HEIGHT	1.88 M (6 FT 2 IN)
RETIRED	1995

Our first Scotsman on the list and a player that just couldn't have been left off it, Gavin Hastings was cut from the same cloth as players like Serge Blanco and David Campese. He was a fullback who was just as dangerous attacking as he was defending. He was granite but had an attacking flair and superb kicking record that made him invaluable to both his country and the British Lions.

We have had some families in this book who have produced several top-class players, and none more successfully than the Hastings. Gavin's brother Scott played for Scotland and the Lions, and his son, Adam, currently plays for Gloucester and Scotland. All of them were class, but Gavin was exceptional.

Andrew Gavin Hastings was born in Edinburgh on 3 January 1962. His younger brother came along three years later, and they quickly discovered their love of rugby. Gavin attended George Watson's College in his hometown and then the Paisley College of Technology (now the University of the West of Scotland). He excelled in rugby throughout his time there, but it really took off once he started at Magdalene College in Cambridge.

He captained most of the teams he played for in his youth career, including the Scottish Schoolboys, who he led to a famous victory over their arch-rivals,

England. He finished his education with a BA in Land Economy in 1986.

Gavin played at a time when rugby was mostly an international sport. There were clubs and provincial teams, of course, but it wasn't professional. In fact, Gavin finished up around the time the sport went professional in 1996. He was still turning out occasionally for London Scottish, but his career was winding down.

Even though Gavin was three years older than his brother, they actually made their Scotland debut in the same game. It came against France at Murrayfield Stadium in 1986, and Gavin scored a then-record six penalties in a superb 18–17 win. It had only taken him one game to show the world of rugby how good his kicking was, and he did it in style.

That same year, he scored five penalties and three conversions in a 33–6 demolition of England. It was another record and a massive result in the history of the Scotland-England rivalry. The two Hastings were quickly becoming Scottish legends, and they were only in their early twenties!

Gavin was a major part of the British Lions' successful tour of Australia in 1989. Scott played in that team, too, but it was Gavin who stole the show. He finished the tour as the top scorer, his kicking especially impressive. Gavin's scoring for the Lions continued throughout his career, and he is still their record points scorer (66).

At a time when fullbacks rarely ventured forward,

Gavin Hastings broke all the rules. He loved to change defence into attack, and this was never more evident when he scored relentlessly at the 1995 World Cup. What makes it even more impressive is that Gavin was nearing the end of his career at the time.

His final game for his nation came in that World Cup against New Zealand in the quarterfinals. In an epic game that saw Scott scoring a try and Gavin kicking three conversions and three penalties, Scotland were just pipped by the Kiwis. Gavin's high scoring at that World Cup made him the tournament's all-time highest scorer, a record he held until it was beaten by Jonny Wilkinson.

In total, Gavin played 61 times for Scotland, scoring a then-record 667 points. He was also a leader on the field and captained his side for 20 of those 61 Tests. He played for several Edinburgh district teams and some other clubs, including London Scottish and the Barbarians in New Zealand. He also appeared in the Hong Kong Sevens.

After hanging up his rugby boots, he tried his hand at American football. He signed for the Scottish Claymores in 1996 as a kicker, helping them to the World Bowl* at Murrayfield Stadium, the home of Scottish rugby! He retired after that before moving to the media side of things, where his charm made him one of Britain's most loved sportspeople.

Gavin Hastings has always been known as a gentleman, and his leadership skills and faultless kicking made him possibly Scotland's greatest-ever player. Like Campese and Blanco, he must also be credited for what he did to evolve the game. People like these guys are mavericks, and without them, every sport would stay the same forever.

Since 2001, he has been the patron of the Sandpaper Trust, a charity organisation that provides medical supplies for struggling neighbourhoods. He was awarded an Order of the British Empire (OBE) in 1993 for his services to rugby and was inducted into the International Rugby Hall of Fame in 2003 and then the World Rugby Hall of Fame a decade later.

There haven't been many players like Gavin Hastings. Scotland fans still sing his name to this day, and we think that tells us everything we need to know about the man. If you haven't seen him play, check out his highlight reels on YouTube! What a player. What a guy!

PERCY
MONTGOMERY

INTERNATIONAL CAREER	
DEBUT	1997
CAPS	102
WINS	67
TRIES	25
POINTS	893

WORLD CUP STATS	
DEBUT	1999
TOURNAMENTS	2
TRIES	2
POINTS	111
TITLES	1

BIOGRAPHY

BORN	15 MARCH 1974
NATIONALITY	SOUTH AFRICAN
POSITION(S)	FULLBACK, CENTRE, FLYHALF
HEIGHT	1.85 M (6 FT 1 IN)
RETIRED	2009

Fullback, centre, fly-half—it made no difference where Percy Montgomery played. He always performed superbly. There could have been no other way for a man who went on to play more Tests for South Africa than any other player and to become their record points scorer. Percy is also a World Cup winner, and even though his club career wasn't as glamorous as some, he was a legend of the game who continues to be credited with reinventing the way players kick.

Apart from his near-perfect kicking, massive size and defensive prowess, Percy had an electric burst of pace. He was a rock at the back and a constant danger going forward. He drove his team on, and that's why he is so highly regarded today.

Percy was born in Walvis Bay, Namibia, on 15 March 1974. He attended the South African College School in Cape Town as a boy, a school known for producing many top sportspeople. It is one of the oldest schools in the whole of Africa, and Percy thrived there, especially in sports.

He was snapped up at an early age as word of his talents spread. His early years were spent playing for Western Province in the Currie Cup and the Stormers in Super Rugby. Pretty soon, his speed and kicking were being talked about, and the Springboks began to take notice.

It was at international level that Percy would make his name. Although he won Currie Cups during his provincial career, club trophies were rare. But wherever he played, he was usually the best player in the team.

Percy's South Africa debut couldn't have been harder. In July 1997, he was thrown to the Lions, literally! He had to play his first Springboks game against the British & Irish Lions during their tour of South Africa. He was played as an outside centre and really impressed. In fact, after that, he was rarely out of the first XV.

Well, that's not entirely true. There were periods when he wasn't in the South Africa team, but that was due to silly rules and a moment of madness. The first of these issues was the rule that meant players who played their club rugby outside of South Africa couldn't be selected for the national team. Percy had signed for Welsh side Newport in 2002, so he became unavailable for the Springboks.

Thankfully for South African rugby, the rule was torn up in 2004.

The other thing that affected his international career was his own fault. It came in a game for Newport when he lost his head and pushed a line judge to the ground. He was banned for 18 months, which kept him out of the 2003 World Cup. Doing something so silly was very unlike Percy, but he learned from his mistake.

Everyone makes mistakes, but we should always learn from them as Percy did. The best thing we can do is try to do better the next time!

When the ban on players playing outside of South Africa was lifted in 2004, newly appointed Springboks coach Jake White instantly recalled Percy. That teamed him with other superstars like Bryan Habana and Schalk Burger. With Habana's try-scoring and Montgomery's kicking, South Africa were becoming a force to be reckoned with.

Now that he was back in the team, Percy picked up where he left off. He was the top point scorer in the 2004 Tri Nations, helping South Africa win the tournament. He repeated this feat the following year, and even though the Springboks didn't retain their Tri Nations title, the team was really starting to gel.

Even with the rule change that allowed him to play abroad and still be selected for South Africa, Percy moved back to the southern hemisphere in 2006 to play for the Sharks. He wanted to be fully prepared for the upcoming World Cup. While with the Sharks, he played several different positions, which helped keep him sharp. It was while he was there that he came closest to winning the Super 14 (Super Rugby) title, barely missing out as the Sharks finished as runners-up.

But those mid-2000 years were immense for Percy Montgomery. In 2006, he became the first Springbok player to reach 600 points, and a few months before the 2007 World Cup, he reached 700! And the milestones* kept coming. At the World Cup, in a match against England in the pool stage, he hit the 800-point mark while also equalling Joost van der

Westhuizen's 89 Test appearance record! He surpassed the appearance record in the following match against Tonga.

As we know, South Africa went on to lift the trophy, winning their second World Cup. Percy was the tournament's top points scorer, and his teammate Bryan Habana scored the most tries. They were a fantastic side that will go down in history, and rightly so. Not many teams have such immense defensive qualities while also being one of the best attacking sides.

Oh, and that pool game where Percy equalled the Test cap record and hit 800 points? The team also embarrassed the English with an astounding 36-0 win! Following the World Cup, Percy moved back to the northern hemisphere, joining Perpignan. He played one season of Top 14 rugby before moving back to the Stormers and Western Province in 2008.

Percy's 100th Test cap was a bittersweet moment. It was such a proud achievement, but it was marred by the fact that his team lost to New Zealand. He made up for it, though, as his final Test cap came in a 53–8 demolition of rivals Australia. Percy quickly moved into coaching, becoming South Africa's kicking consultant, and he retired soon after.

Outside of rugby, he is a successful businessman and philanthropist*, and it is only a matter of time before he is inducted into every Hall of Fame in rugby. To play a record number of times for South Africa takes some doing. To become their record points scorer with more than double that of the man in second place is simply unreal.

Will there ever be another Springboks player like Percy Montgomery? Probably not. He was truly one of a kind!

GARETH EDWARDS

INTERNATIONAL CAREER

DEBUT	1967
CAPS	53
TRIES	20
GRAND SLAMS	3
FIVE NATIONS TITLES	7

CLUB CAREER

DEBUT	1966
CAPS	195
TRIES	69
POINTS	426

BORN	12 JULY 1947
NATIONALITY	WELSH
POSITION(S)	SCRUM-HALF
HEIGHT	1.73 M (5 FT 8 IN)
RETIRED	1978

Back in the late sixties and early seventies, one nation dominated European rugby, and that team was Wales. In what is considered the greatest backline of all time, Gareth Edwards was the leader and best of a fantastic bunch. During that remarkable period, Wales won the Five Nations a staggering 11 times in 16 years with Edwards at scrum half.

Life wasn't easy for Gareth growing up. He was born into a mining family in Gwaun-Cae-Gurwen, Glamorgan, Wales, two years after World War II. Britain was still in a state of devastation, and most families struggled to make ends meet. The Edwards were no different, and the kids often went hungry. Rugby became an escape for young Gareth, and it led to a fantastic career.

Gareth attended Pontardawe School for Boys (now called Cwmtawe Community School) as a kid. It was there that he met a very important person in his life. That man was one of his teachers, Bill Samuels. Bill saw something in Gareth, and he encouraged him to use his talents to the best of his ability. Gareth excelled in several different sports, including gymnastics, athletics, rugby and football.

In fact, he was so good at the last of these that he was called up to the West Wales youth team. This led to a contract offer from Swansea City when Gareth was 16.

But he always preferred rugby, even though there was a lot more money and fame in football.

Gareth signed for Cardiff RFC straight out of school, and he stayed there for his whole club career. He made his debut in September 1966 and went on to play 195 games over 12 seasons. Despite playing in their back line, he managed to score 69 tries. He was another one of our mavericks—a player who reinvented the game!

His first game for Wales came in April 1967 at the age of 19 against France in Paris. It ended in a 14–20 loss, but the signs were there that Wales were building something great. Over the next decade or so, they would become a force to be reckoned with. Also, from that point on, Gareth played nonstop for his country. And we mean nonstop.

From that game in 1967 to his final game in 1978, Gareth didn't miss one of Wales' matches. Not one. He was never dropped and never injured. Of all the records in rugby, that has to be one of the most impressive.

One year after his debut, Gareth became Wales' youngest-ever captain at the age of just 20. That unreal backline was starting to gel, and they impressed again, restricting Scotland to exactly no points in a 5–0 Welsh victory. His partnership with Barry John and Phil Bennett was really taking off.

Gareth had an especially strong bond with Barry John, and they often seemed to have a telepathic* relationship on the field. With the Welsh backline at their peak, a golden era began. They won several Five

Nations Grand Slams in that ridiculous run of 11 in 16, with Edwards often seen as the superstar. His ability to turn defence into attack obliterated teams and a domination of the home nations was formed that has yet to be equalled.

His time with the British & Irish Lions was also successful. Gareth was part of the Lions team that became the first to win a series in New Zealand in 1971 and the one that went unbeaten in 1974 in their series against South Africa.

Personal awards soon started to come. He won the BBC Sports Personality of the Year in 1974, and he was awarded an MBE* the following year. Normally, such honours as an MBE are given to people at the end of their career, but Gareth was so exceptional that he earned it while still playing.

Gareth's international career came to an end like it began: against France, only this time, Wales won. At the Cardiff Arms Park, in front of 60,000 people, Wales beat the French 16–7, with Edwards scoring a drop goal. Wales won the Five Nations and the Triple Crown, the last of these for the third time in a row. Gareth walked away from the game a champion, which was how it was always going to be. He was a natural winner.

As expected, he was in that group of 15 former players inducted into the inaugural* International Rugby Hall of Fame. He received this honour with his two ex-teammates, Barry John and JPR Williams. In 2001, he was named the Greatest Welsh Player of All Time, and he was knighted a few years later.

While playing for the Barbarians against New Zealand at Cardiff Arms Park in 1973, Gareth scored what is simply known as "That Try." With a name like that, it's clear to see why it is often considered the greatest try ever scored. Of course, Jonah Lomu probably wouldn't have agreed after his demolition job against England, but that's the beauty of sport—we can make up our own minds!

If you haven't seen it, look it up! You can thank us later.

Just like in his school days, Gareth continued to excel in many sports following his retirement. In 1990, he broke the British angling* record when he caught a 45-pound 6-ounce pike! He held the record for two years. He is active in many different charities and has appeared on several game shows through the years.

In a 2003 poll in Rugby World magazine, Gareth Edwards was voted the greatest player of all time. To the Welsh fans, there is no question that this is a fact, and a lot of other fans would agree.

Sir Gareth Edwards was the main cog in the machine that was the greatest backline in history. He was immense, and his dominance with Wales will surely never be equalled.

JPR WILLIAMS

INTERNATIONAL CAREER

DEBUT	1969
CAPS	55
WINS	37
TRIES	6
POINTS	36

INTERNATIONAL HONOURS

GRAND SLAMS	3
TRIPLE CROWNS	6
CAPS AS CAPTAIN	5

BIOGRAPHY

BORN	2 MARCH 1949
NATIONALITY	WELSH
POSITION(S)	FULL BACK
HEIGHT	1.85 M (6 FT 1 IN)
RETIRED	2003

We probably could have put half of that Welsh team that dominated the late sixties and seventies on this list, as they were that good. Instead, we've taken the two who are generally considered to be the best of that exceptional group. We've just had Sir Gareth Edwards, and now we have one of his partners in crime, Mr John Peter Rhys Williams.

JPR Williams wasn't just a world-class fullback who could also play as a flanker or fly-half; he was one of the first rugby players to become an international icon. With his flowing hair, long sideburns and socks around his ankles, he was rugby's George Best.

But JPR wasn't simply a rugby player. This guy could do everything. Throughout his career, he became a doctor, then a surgeon, and he was even a top tennis player in his youth. In fact, he won a junior competition at Wimbledon, beating a young David Lloyd, who would go on to win 14 professional titles!

JPR actually chose rugby because it was an amateur sport at the time, and he wanted to make sure his medical training was never interrupted. He wanted to heal people, so medicine came first!

John Peter Rhys Williams was born in Bridgend, Wales, on 2 March 1949, at a tough time for Britain. Like his future teammate Gareth Edwards, he grew up in post-World War II Britain. Times were hard, and sports became an escape for most kids. JPR was no different, and he soon had the rugby bug!

He attended Millfield School as a kid, which just so happened to be the same school as his future teammate Gareth Edwards! He was a few years behind Gareth, so they didn't play youth rugby together, but we think it's fair to say that whoever coached the kids at Millfield deserves an award!

He continued his education and studied medicine at St Mary's Hospital Medical School. During this period, he played rugby union for London Welsh, and it was there that he was discovered by the Wales national team scouts. He was called up soon after and made his Test debut in 1969 at just 19.

His dynamic style and flash appearance made him an instant favourite in the dressing room, and the backline he became part of meant the fans adored him. He broke into the Wales team just as they were starting to dominate, and some people see him as the final piece in the puzzle.

One of JPR's proudest achievements is his record against arch-rivals England. In 10 Test matches against the old enemy, he scored five tries, which is unbelievable for a fullback. On top of that, JPR was never once on the losing side!

While he was dominating for Wales in the seventies, he also turned out for his local cricket team. Add to that his career as a doctor, and you clearly have a man who likes to keep busy. There were also the British

Lions tours to be played. JPR played a significant role in the Lions' famous 1971 and '74 tours of New Zealand and South Africa.

Amazingly, he became a fully qualified orthopaedic* surgeon in between those tours, somehow finding the time to do it all at once.

Another one of JPR's skills was his jumping. His ability to leap higher than everyone else, his hair flowing in the wind, and come down with the ball safely in his grasp was legendary. After a tour of Argentina with Wales, the locals gave him the nickname "The Bucket" due to the way the ball seemed to sink into his body when he caught it.

Along with Gareth Edwards, JPR played an important role in "That Try." Edwards gets the plaudits* for scoring the try, but it was JPR's exceptional work in the leadup that made it all possible.

With his medical career becoming busier every year, JPR often had to wind his rugby career back. He knew that a serious injury could impact his skills as a surgeon, so he had to be careful. His true passion was helping people, and he didn't want to lose that ability. This was the case when he turned down the chance to travel to New Zealand for a Lions tour in 1977.

He did continue to play, but mostly for local clubs. Remember, he was also turning out for the Lord's Taverners cricket team as well! But his love of sports would never leave him, and while he continued to be a top surgeon, he actually played rugby and cricket on some level into his 50s! Yes, that's right... his 50s!

Although he retired from Test rugby in 1981, he played on with his hometown club, Bridgend, into the late nineties. After that, he joined the Tondu Thirds and played there until he was 54, finally retiring from all forms of rugby in 2003! His cricket career was even longer, and it wasn't until the following year that he stopped stepping up to the crease.

But JPR didn't stop there. He still needed action, and he combined this energy with another of his passions —his charity work—in 2006 when he climbed Mount Kilimanjaro to raise money for the NSPCC*. At 55 years of age, he did what most people 30 years younger wouldn't dream of attempting. He raised over £200,000.

Alongside his old teammates Gareth Edwards and Barry John, he was part of the inaugural 15 players inducted into the International Rugby Hall of Fame.

This list might have all 20 players in no particular order (it would be impossible to separate them all), but it's still kind of fitting that JPR Williams tops it off. A man who reached the top of his game while studying and practising as a surgeon deserves so much praise. Who knows how good he would have been if he had concentrated solely on rugby? We would probably have to make him his own list!

FINAL WHISTLE

So, we've come to the end of our journey through 20 of rugby's most legendary players. Of course, there were some players who probably deserved a place in our book, but the final 20 has to end somewhere! For those who missed out, we can only apologise. But that's the beauty of being a sports fan, right? We get to debate, discuss and even argue sometimes over who we think is the best. There is no right or wrong answer. It's whoever we believe it to be.

It happens in every sport. Is Ronaldo better than Messi? And even if he is, maybe Maradona is better than both of them! Would Muhammad Ali have beaten Mike Tyson if both fighters were in their prime, and what would happen if a young John McEnroe played Roger Federer? Nobody can truly say who's the greatest.

What would Sergio Parisse's medal collection look like if he'd played for New Zealand? It would surely be much bigger, yet he would be the exact same player. So, it's unfair to judge him simply on his trophy haul, right? That's why some of the players on our list earned their spots in different ways.

The same goes for those guys who played back when there were no European trophies for clubs or even a professional domestic league. How can they be judged against a modern-day player who gets to compete in the Investec Champions Cup (formerly the Heineken Cup) every year? As you will have seen, a lot of the earlier players had to work everyday jobs on the side to make ends meet, so they didn't play in as many tournaments.

But one thing every player on this list has in common is that they all made the sport of rugby better. Most of them changed the way people see it, from Percy Montgomery's and Jonny Wilkinson's kicking styles to Jonah Lomu proving that a man of immense size can still be compared to a ballerina because they are so nimble!

Rugby is a brutal sport, but it's always been played with a huge amount of class. Unlike football and other such sports, you won't see a rugby player trying to con the referee. When they get hit hard, they shake it off and carry on. And when the ref speaks, every player keeps quiet and listens. In these ways, rugby is unique. Its core values have remained the same since 1823, when a young William Webb Ellis first picked the ball up during a game of football and ran the length of the field.

Rugby was invented that day, and it's no coincidence that the man who created it still has his name on the Rugby World Cup trophy. The Webb Ellis Cup is a symbol of everything that is good about the sport. For those who get to lift it, it's often the greatest moment in their lives. For others, it's only a dream.

Of course, some of the players in this book never even got a chance to compete at the Rugby World Cup, as it didn't begin until 1987. For them, it was the Tri Nations, the Five (later Six) Nations, Lions tours, and friendly internationals that gave them their chances at greatness. How would that Wales team of the seventies have fared in a World Cup? It's hard to imagine that they wouldn't have won at least one if it had been around at the time.

Still, Sir Gareth Edwards and JPR Williams are legends of the game without ever having played at a World Cup. They are remembered because they were simply sensational. The same goes for all our legends of rugby!

And we hope you enjoyed learning about them all. Thanks to modern technology, there is footage of almost all of them online, so look them up. They all had their own style, and looking back over moments like "That Try" and Jonah Lomu's demolition of England will never get boring!

GLOSSARY

Angling - The sport of fishing.

Azzurri - Italian term for "Blues" used for most of the country's sports teams.

Baptism of fire - A tough start to something.

Bums on seats - An old saying meaning a player, singer, team, etc., who gets people into stadiums due to their talents.

CBE - Commander of Order of the British Empire. An award for people who help Britain from back home rather than the frontline during a war.

Flamboyant - Someone with flair or flash skills or who stands out.

Humanitarian - A person who goes the extra mile to help others, usually through charity work.

Inaugural - The start of or first of something, usually a competition or the beginning of a business.

Latter - The second of two points, with the first being the "former".

Liability - A person or thing who is likely to cause an issue.

MBE - Member of the Most Excellent Order of the British Empire. The third highest rank of the Order of the British Empire.

Milestone - An important event or stage in an achievement or career.

NSPCC - National Society for the Prevention of Cruelty to Children.

Orthopaedic - The treatment and correction of bones and muscles.

Philanthropist - Someone who does a lot for charity.

Plaudits - Credit and praise.

Pundits - People who commentate or criticise their chosen sport.

Ranfurly Shield - Sometimes called the Log o' Wood, it is one of the oldest domestic trophies in rugby. It is a domestic trophy in New Zealand.

Revolutionary - A person who changes something or reinvents a part of it.

Sabbatical - An agreed-to break for a period of time (usually while still being paid).

Sporadic - Something that happens irregularly.

Staying power - Able to last or play or keep the same high standards for a long period of time.

Telepathic - The myth of being able to pass thoughts between two or more human beings.

Tier One rugby - Usually considered the highest quality teams, including all of the Six Nations teams and the big four in the southern hemisphere: Australia, New Zealand, Argentina and South Africa.

Wooden Spoon Society - A brilliant charity organisation that helps kids with disabilities or who grow up disadvantaged.

World Bowl - The European version of America's Super Bowl.

Printed in Great Britain
by Amazon

35536203R00066